THE ISLAND SERIES

GRAND BAHAMA

THE ISLAND SERIES

†Harris and Lewis
The Isle of Arran
†The Isle of Mull
Lundy
The Maltese Islands
†Orkney
St Kilda and other Hebridean Outliers
*Corsica
*Vancouver Island
*The Falkland Islands
†Shetland
*Singapore

in preparation
*The Seychelles
*Singapore
*The Solomon Islands
Canary Islands: Fuerteventura
and many others

* Published in the United States by Stackpole
† Published in the United States by David & Charles

GRAND BAHAMA

by P. J. H. BARRATT

DAVID & CHARLES : NEWTON ABBOT
STACKPOLE BOOKS : HARRISBURG

This edition first published in 1972
in Great Britain by David & Charles (Publishers) Limited
Newton Abbot Devon
in the United States by Stackpole Books
Harrisburg Pa.

ISBN 0 7153 5655 0 (*Great Britain*)
ISBN 0–8117–0751–2 (*United States*)

*Set in eleven on thirteen point Baskerville
and printed in Great Britain by
Clarke Doble & Brendon Limited Plymouth
for David & Charles (Publishers) Limited
South Devon House   Newton Abbot   Devon*

To the young Bahamians
Anne-Marie, Margot and Paulette

CONTENTS

		Page
1	Island of the Great Shallows	13
2	Geology, Climate and Natural History . .	23
3	Discovery and Oblivion	43
4	Resettlement	60
5	Industry, Bootlegging and Tourism . . .	74
6	The Hawksbill Creek Agreement . . .	91
7	Island on the Move	103
8	Change of Government	115
9	Settlement and Settlers	130
10	Planning of Freeport/Lucaya	142
11	Grand Bahama Today	155

Appendixes:

A An Island Gazetteer	177
B Notes on Place Names	187
Bibliography and Extract of Official Reports, etc., relating to Freeport	191
Acknowledgements	199
Index	201

ILLUSTRATIONS

PLATES

	Page
Bell Channel Bay and city of Freeport *(Clemens)*	17
Grand Lucayan waterway *(Clemens)*	17
Grand Bahama Highway *(Clemens)*	18
Oldest hotel on the island	35
Grand Bahama Hotel *(Ministry of Tourism, Bahamas)*	35
Deluxe Lucayan Beach Hotel *(Clemens)*	36
Taino Beach restaurant *(Clemens)*	53
Golf course at Freeport *(Jualmo Studio)*	53
El Casino at night *(Jualmo Studio)*	54
MV *Freeport*, ferry with mainland *(Clemens)*	54
Lynden O. Pindling, prime minister *(Freeport News)*	71
Jack Hayward *(Clemens)*	71
James Rand *(Clemens)*	71
Signing Hawksbill Creek Agreement *(Bahamas Government)*	72
Central Freeport *(GBPA)*	72
Joseph Bevin, octogenarian	89
Mrs Bevin, smoking	89
Drusila Laing with turtle	89
Junkanoo drummer *(Clemens)*	89
Arawak Indian girl *(Dr Albury)*	90
Anglican church, Freeport *(Clemens)*	107
Roman Catholic church, Seagrape	107
Hermitage former Baptist church	107
Cement silos *(GBPA)*	108
Ships bunkering and oil refinery *(Clemens)*	108
'Pieces of eight' *(Clemens)*	125
Freeport Power Company plant *(Clemens)*	125
Lumber Company railway *(Leo Savola)*	126
Telemetry installation *(Clemens)*	126
Street in Spanish section *(Clemens)*	143
Churchill Square, Freeport *(Clemens)*	143

ILLUSTRATIONS

	Page
Curly-tailed lizard *(Clemens)*	144
'Boiling' hole near 'Old' Freetown *(Clemens)* . . .	144

MAPS

The Caribbean	15
The Bahama Islands *(Donald Dean)*	21
Grand Bahama *(H. Williams)*	*pull out inside back cover*

DIAGRAMS

Typical section through the island *(R. Pilfold)* . . .	24
Population graph *(R. Pilfold)*	156
Annual number of visitors *(GBPA)*	158
Hotel rooms in Grand Bahama *(GBPA)* . . .	159
Motor vehicles *(Bahamas Government)*	161
Electricity consumers *(Freeport Power Company)* .	164
Government revenue from Freeport area *(Bahamas Government)*	166

NOTE ON CURRENCY

All sums of money quoted in this book are in United States dollars which are valued at 95 cents to the Bahamian dollar (1972) and are worth approximately 39 pence. (£1 = $2.50.) (Prior to 1967, pounds, shillings and pence were used in the Bahamas.)

1   ISLAND OF THE GREAT SHALLOWS

ON 3 August 1492 an almost unknown Genoese sailor, armed with a concession from the Spanish Crown to take possession of 'certain islands and mainland in the western ocean', set sail from the tiny seaport of Palos, in Spain, on an adventure which would galvanise western civilisation. Christopher Columbus proceeded from Palos to the Canary Islands, then the last outpost of Mediterranean civilisation. There he took on provisions, made structural repairs and directed the re-rigging of one of his ships.

Due west, on the same latitude, lay Grand Bahama Island, and it was a due west course that he set. Halfway across the Atlantic, partly because of a change of winds, the tiny convoy of three ships altered course more southward. As a result, on 10 October Columbus made a landfall on the southeastern Bahamian island which he promptly christened San Salvador (Holy Saviour). Undoubtedly, the practical man of the sea was moved, not so much by his piety as by his need to please his fervent patroness Queen Isabella the Catholic.

The political implications of his discovery are important. The natives that Columbus met directed him southwestwardly again and, after sailing through the southern Bahamas for another two weeks, he discovered the large islands of Hispaniola and Cuba, and, on a later voyage, South America. If, however, he had remained on the course he had set originally on leaving the Canary Islands he would have discovered Grand Bahama and, by completing his voyage by crossing the narrow straits to the west, he would certainly have claimed North America for the Spanish Crown.

On approaching the islands Columbus wrote that what he saw was 'so uncertain a thing he did not wish to declare it was land'. Indeed the highest point of San Salvador is barely over 100ft and the highest elevation of the northern Bahama island of Grand Bahama is a mere 60ft above sea level—hardly conspicuous features to an anxious mariner searching the horizon for a landfall. From five miles out at sea Grand Bahama cannot be seen, and it is only on drawing closer that a hazy line appears on the horizon; nearer, breakers may appear on an off-shore reef, and nearer still shallows are encountered. Understandably, the Spanish explorers noted with consternation the extensive shallows and the island became known as *Gran bajamar* (the great shallows; literally : the vast underwater). Later the country took its name from the island.

Interest in the northern islands of the Bahamas goes back to shortly after the arrival of Columbus in the Indies. The legendary *Fountain of Youth* was sought by the Spanish explorer Ponce de León in this region; but if he, or anybody else, found it they kept it a closely guarded secret. Some would even suggest that the legendary country of *Atlantis* is located in the northern Bahamas, but evidence to support this claim is slender. Nevertheless in the years following the landfall of Columbus many explorations were made of the region though no attempt was made by the Spaniards at settlement.

Grand Bahama is the most northerly of the stepping-stone islands which almost form a land bridge between Florida and Venezuela. It is the fourth largest of the Bahama Islands and is situated at its nearest point a mere 55 miles from Florida on the opposite side of the Florida Channel. It has an area of some 530 square miles and is 70 miles in length from east to west and about 9 miles across at its widest girth. To the south and west of the island lies the deep water of the Northwest Providence Channel and the Gulf Stream respectively and to the north is a semi-circular-shaped shallow which extends for about 60 miles to the Manatilla Shoal.

Since the centuries following Ponce de León's discovery of

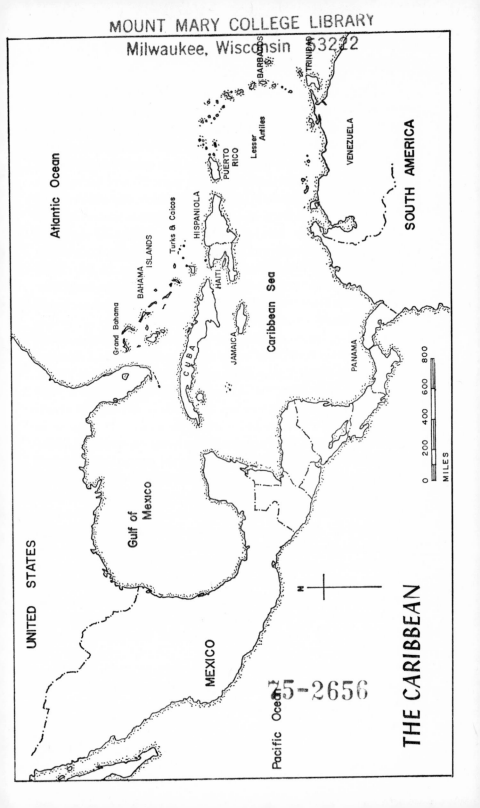

THE CARIBBEAN

Grand Bahama have left us a paucity of first-hand recorded history, we must infer that the island played some typical, if small, part in the evolution of the Island-Commonwealth; in fact it is quite possible that only in the last few years has the population of Grand Bahama exceeded that of four centuries ago. Indeed, before the arrival of Columbus there were thought to be about 40,000 Lucayan Indians in the Bahamas which, by a rough apportionment, would indicate that there were 4,000 on Grand Bahama alone. Not until the 1953 Bahama Islands Census did the island record over that number of inhabitants. Though the Lucayans of the islands were quite primitive, they enjoyed a tranquil, almost utopian, life-style insulated from the brutalities of harsher climes. Sir Thomas More, the philosopher of 'ideal' communities, would certainly have admired the Lucayans' 'commonweal' and it is interesting to recall that Sir Thomas set his Utopia on an island not so very different in size and shape from Grand Bahama.

After the Spanish conquistadores the island was seldom visited. But since early times the existence of the island has been well known and, though it was never settled, it appears on almost every chart of the West Indies which shows the 27° parallel. In the last few years, however, due to the rapid development principally centred on Freeport, it has become the second most populous of the Bahama Islands. Since the island is only two hours away from New York and half an hour away from Miami by jet aeroplane, Grand Bahama today is readily accessible. On approaching the island by air it is not always clear where the land begins and the sea ends, and if this ambiguity exists to the airborne passenger, it is even more true for the mariner. For, after its discovery by the Spaniards, the island—or more correctly the reefs off the island—has been a graveyard for galleons, men-of-war, merchantmen and passenger ships. It is easy to understand why the island had never attracted visitors—it was a good place to avoid!

When the island was finally settled, the new communities were located close to the shoreline, almost every house being within sight of the sea. The interior of the island was never actually

Page 17 The island from the air: (above) Bell Channel Bay which was once swashland. Across the channel the Lucayan Beach Hotel can be seen. The city of Freeport is in the upper right of the picture; (below) Grand Lucayan waterway, looking north. The Hermitage is on Barbary Beach at bottom right

Page 18 Grand Bahama Highway, looking east and showing part of the Grand Lucayan waterway

settled though it was opened up by the lumber operations which worked the island from time to time. It is almost true to say that every square foot of the island has been explored by the gangs of lumbermen who cut down the Bahamian pine and shipped it all over the world. Some of the lumber ended up as wooden siding on houses in Cuba, some as ceiling joists in the West Indies and some as pit props hundreds of feet down in the earth in coal seams of the Black Country and Northumberland. Even before lumber companies worked the island there were selective cuttings made of mahogany and dyewood trees; and Grand Bahama's straight lofty pines provided Bahamian sloops with many a mast and spar.

The natural beauty of the island can best be seen on the south coast beaches generally away from the settled areas. From any coppice of beach trees can be seen a lambent blue-green ocean, a powder-white sand beach and, as a frame to the picture, branches of seagrape, cocoa plum and orange love vine. This view of the island is a common one, yet it is similar to that observed by the first man to set foot on the island nearly three millennia ago; and this is only the surface of the picture. Below the sea there is another world almost impossible to imagine from the vantage point of the shore. Equipped with underwater apparatus the adventurous can see underwater mountains, grotesque coral forms and a myriad variety of fish and other marine life in the gin-clear waters.

Inland the hand of man has generally enhanced nature by creating a network of shimmering waterways and the scenery is probably at its best where pine forests have been cleared to create the fairways for numerous golf courses. Some delightful vistas have been opened up to the eye, and besides the natural hazards of the coppice to a sliced drive, bunkers and lakes also serve at once to please and infuriate the hapless golfer. Even the giant cement plant and refinery form an industrial landscape which has a visual impact, if not a beauty of its own. And as day draws to a close an unforgettable experience is to watch the scarlet sun descend to the treetops, lighting from beneath a dizzily coloured herringbone sky and then, all too rapidly, sink visibly behind the pine barren and into the sea.

A less usual view of the island is that seen from the swash-land of the north shore. Though not conveniently accessible the mangrove-covered shallows have that rare kind of beauty which naturalists so love. In the unearthly stillness only the birdlife punctuates the silence. The tidal flats teem with small fish which seek the safety of shallow water in infancy before joining the battle of life on the Bank.

Unlike the more developed Bahama Islands such as New Providence (on which Nassau, the capital, is situated), Eleuthera and Harbour Island, there is no lack of 'growing room' on Grand Bahama. At the relatively low density of 100 persons per square mile the island could support half a million people and research has shown that at the present rate of water consumption the needs of such a population could be satisfied. In addition, the island has important natural resources, in its climate, its beaches and in the thick forest of pine trees which almost covers the entire island. A further important natural resource is the particularly pure limestone of which the island is formed which is the basic material of the cement industry.

Grand Bahama is now part of the newly emergent nation known officially as the Commonwealth of the Bahama Islands, though a portion of the island enjoys a special status conferred by the Hawksbill Creek Agreement, signed in 1955, which led to the creation of Freeport. It is strange however, in light of the advantages the island afforded, that development did not take place sooner; certainly Grand Bahama's geographical location and resources would have made eventual flowering inevitable. Its proximity to the North American continent, long history of political stability, resident work force, minimal taxation, year-round mild climate, ample quantities of potable water, together with large tracts of inexpensive land available for purchase from the Crown, all begged development.

From its beginnings the people associated with the island have represented the full spectrum of races. The early inhabitants ethnic-

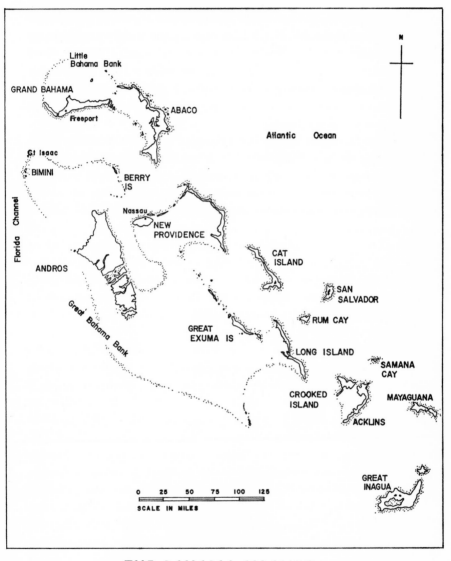

THE BAHAMA ISLANDS

ally belonged to the 'yellow' race—kin to the Red Indian of America; the Europeans, broadly classified as 'white', were in fact olive-skinned Spaniards and pink-complexioned Englishmen; later came the 'black' Africans who ranged in colour from ebony to light chocolate. Today the whole spectrum of races, colours and creeds cohabit the island in unusual harmony. Yet with all these factors favouring development, it is surprising that it was not until 1948 that anybody seriously attempted to exploit the potential of the island. In that year Billy (later Sir Billy) Butlin started work on a large hotel complex and holiday village at the west end of the island; and a decade later Wallace Groves dredged a harbour at the mouth of Hawksbill Creek, which formed a basis for development of the island's interior, and subsequently for a whole 'new world' being created on Grand Bahama.

Prayer for Provincial Elections

Creator God, we praise you for
all your marvelous works among
us and for the many gifts and
blessings that have brought us
to this moment in our history.
Grant us insight and wisdom as
we discern the needs of our
province and search for
sisters who will lead us in
carrying out our mission.
"Give us your Holy Spirit, who
alone can free our hearts in love." (MT)
Enable us as true daughters of
Blessed Theresa and Mother
Caroline to be attentive to
your will, ready to do
whatever Jesus tells us. Amen.

2   GEOLOGY, CLIMATE AND NATURAL HISTORY

PHYSICAL GEOGRAPHY

G RAND BAHAMA is located in the western Atlantic Ocean at north latitude 26° 31′ and west longitude 78° 44′. Geographically the island, together with Little and Great Abaco Islands, are exposed portions of the Little Bahama Bank.

The island is topographically uninteresting, the highest point being only 60ft above sea level. A typical section through the island originally showed a swamp near the southern coral sand shore, a low ridge further inland, from which there is an almost indiscernible slope down to the north coast, and then miles of swashland before the sea is reached. The beach on the south shore is composed of sifted coral sand which has been continually washed and further eroded by the action of the sea. The north shore is composed of calcareous muds, limes, and clays. These white marl beds support thousands of acres of mangroves and other swamp-type vegetation. Inland, beneath a canopy of pines and scrub vegetation, broken limerock is almost everywhere visible on the surface. Organic topsoil is occasionally found in the forested areas as a product of biological decay but despite a thin cover of mosses and ferns the rock is seldom more than a few inches below the surface. Here and there fairly luxuriant vegetation is supported on the rich organic loam found in the occasional 'banana hole' though most of the agriculture since the early times took place in the loamy coral sands slightly inland from the dunes of the south shore.

A series of sloughs bisect the island with water-filled creeks

23

extending quite deep from the north coast inland. Hawksbill Creek is the most conspicuous of these inlets but other examples are found in the eastern half of the island culminating in the creeks separating the cays (small islets pronounced 'keys') which give the map of Grand Bahama the appearance of a lobster tail. Towards the western end of the island the Bahama stoney loam, which supports the pine barren, gives way to Bahama marl and 'swashland'. The cays of the north shore and the eastern tip of the island are mainly mangrove-covered marl beds.

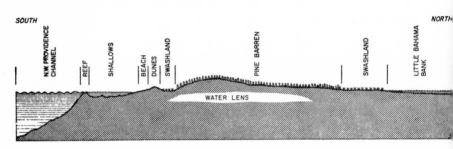

Typical section through the island

GEOLOGY

The northern banks of the Bahama Islands, together with the Florida peninsula and its continental shelf, act as a submarine barrier between the Atlantic Ocean and the Gulf of Mexico. From the shelf has arisen the archipelago of Bahama Islands. Of the three classifications of rocks—igneous, metamorphic and sedimentary—only the latter is represented in the northern Bahamas. Thus rocks created by heat or pressure are unknown in Grand Bahama. Sedimentary rocks originate from the mechanical or chemical destruction of pre-existing rocks and were deposited either in water or through wind action as aeolian silt. In the case of the Bahamas, wind-blown deposits are prevalent showing strictly horizontal and thus parallel lamination or bedding. The limestone has a high content of fossils especially sea animals and shells. Limestone is a calcareous rock and is formed mainly of calcium carbonate or lime, with varying amounts of impurities, resulting either from the deposition of calcium salts or from the action of lime-secreting organisms. In the Bahamas the limestone is almost entirely made up of fossils or fragments of fossils.

The islands are not, as was once supposed, pure coral islands, but are actually composed of minute ovoid and ellipsoid bodies or oolites, set in a cementateous groundmass. This oolitic limestone was laid down as great wind-blown piles of shells and coral from a million to 75 million years ago since which time the islands have been supplemented by the action of living coral which finds an ideal habitat in the warm shallow waters of the northern Caribbean.

Limestone has the chemical composition $CaCo_3$. It is quite hard, sometimes crystalline, but soft enough to be scratched with a knife; it is of varying porosity and will effervesce when brought into contact with acid, giving off carbon dioxide gas. In the cavities well-developed crystals of calcite occur, when calcium carbonate might be dissolved by circulating waters and redeposited as a calcareous incrustation; or else, where dripping from a roof, such saturated solutions give rise to stalactites.

The bedrock of Grand Bahama consists solely of highly soluble limestone, the morphological features of which are generally known as the 'Karst Phenomenon'. It is owing to this condition that many voids are found in the oatmeal-coloured rock which, together with its softness, discourage the use of Bahamian limestone for building masonry. Occasionally large voids open to the surface of the island and are known as 'ocean holes' or 'sink holes' (the same phenomenon in the sea being called a 'blue hole', 'solution hole' or a 'boiling hole'). One of the largest of these holes is located in the swashland of the north coast some ten miles northeast of Hawksbill Creek. This 'ocean hole' forms an almost perfect circle of about 200ft diameter and, though supposedly 'bottomless', it has recently been plumbed at over 200ft. Many kinds of exotic marine life, real and imagined, live in the hole, among them a giant squid, a patriarchal jewfish, a seacow and (personally observed) a 5ft long nurse shark.

Another interesting hole is to be found on dry land behind 'old' Freetown on the south coast. Discernible from only a few feet away because of the dense brush, this hole measures about 50ft by 30ft across and is a yawning 35ft above the clear water at the bottom. The sides of the hole dumbell inwards with small stalactite formations on the walls, making escape from the water below impossible except by rope or ladder. The hole continues underground in a submerged cave and is almost certainly linked to the sea by labyrinthine underground caverns.

An even more interesting series of holes can be found just fifty yards north of the main highway near the American missile base. Also concealed from view, these holes are not so deep to the water level though there is an 'island' at the bottom of one of the holes which allows access to the water's edge. Several large caves radiate out under water and in the caves fantastic stalactite and stalagmite formations can be seen. Some of the stalactites are 12ft long, suggesting that they were formed between 50,000 and 100,000 years before the sea rose to its present level. In all these holes the water is static except for the almost indiscernible action of the tide. However, at Eight Mile Rock there is a hole that 'boils'. Located on the sea-coast, it is a horseshoe in shape disappearing into a cavern on the landward side into which water flows in or out (depending on the tide) at several hundred gallons per minute. It was believed that prior to the harbour expansion this boiling hole was linked underground to Hawksbill Creek. Certainly in Hawksbill Creek there are numerous boiling holes, one of which was less than a mile away from the Eight Mile Rock hole. From one of these holes in the creek a large cave once ran towards the sea and has been followed by divers for a few hundred feet before it narrowed down, becoming impassable. The same divers also reported seeing stalactite formations in these caverns, which bears out the assumption that the sea was once lower than it is today since stalactite formations do not form under water.

Another geological phenomenon of the island is the 'hammock' or rock outcrop. One such has been preserved in the eastern residential area of the city of Freeport and there is another in the Fortune Hills area of Lucaya. These hammocks stretch for about two miles, forming a fairly straight line in a northeasterly southwesterly direction. The position of both hammocks adds credence to the 'wind-blown' theory of the later formation of the Bahama Islands since the line of the hammock formed a windrow approximately perpendicular to the wind, suggesting that it was formed by a wind-blown pile of shell detritus. Both hammocks are riddled with vertical caves, some as deep as 20ft. The vegetation is unusual too in that it consists of guava trees, sapodilla, clusia (sometimes called the autograph tree) and wild vines. One side of the hammock has an almost vertical face, the base of which is about 10ft above present mean low water. The eroded face of the hammock clearly displays the action of the sea hundreds of thousands of years ago when the glaciers retreated and the ocean was for a time higher than it is today.

CLIMATE

The climate of Grand Bahama is subtropical with a mean temperature range of 66° F in January to 82° F in August. For most of the year the sun shines in an azure blue sky. Cloudiness almost invariably portends rain and sustained overcast days are rare. On average the Cornell Report records that cloudiness is minimum in January and maximum in October. October is also the wettest month with about 10in of rain and the total for the year is around 60in. The relative humidity is generally in the high seventies with a daily range not differing much from 15 per cent. A fairly constant breeze helps to alleviate the effects of the high humidity though almost all business premises and many homes use air-conditioning, especially in summer. Frost is unknown because any invading cold air mass must cross over the warming influence of the Gulf Stream, thereby losing enough of its chilling effect on arrival to push it above freezing point. Once considered a winter tourist venue, the Bahamas nowadays is a year-round resort with little seasonal variation in the number of tourists. Though fairly

27

humid in the summer there is little variation in temperature in the islands. In fact so pleasantly mild is the climate of the Bahamas that a Privy Counsellor of Charles V wrote : 'these islands were called fortunate for the temperate ayre which is in them', and a more recent northern visitor called them 'the isles of perpetual June'.

The island is spared violent atmospheric disturbances except for summer thunderstorms and, very occasionally, a hurricane. A hurricane is a tropical cyclone born in the West Indies, the winds of which have a clock-wise motion. The diameter of a hurricane is usually between 100 and 200 miles with a speed of movement of about 15 miles per hour in a re-curving path. Wind speeds are often 150 miles per hour near the centre, though a strange feature is that the pivotal point of the hurricane is a windless 'eye'. The hurricane season extends from about July to October and the hurricanes are designated alphabetically by female names—presumably to indicate their fickle nature. Serious hurricanes passed through the island in 1926 and 1947 when the high winds were accompanied by some flooding. Normally, however, hurricanes seem to be deflected by the more southerly islands of the Bahamas and those on a generally northerly path tend to veer towards the coast of Florida or out into the Atlantic.

As a silent usher to night the short twilight of the northern Bahamas is dominated by some of the most magnificent sunsets seen anywhere in the world. And at night the Southern Cross can be seen low on the horizon while overhead meteorites enter the earth's atmosphere making a shooting gallery out of the heavens.

OCEAN CURRENTS

The principal current of the Gulf Stream flows between the western end of the island and the Florida peninsula on its way north. The warm shallow water of the Bahamas, which has a surf temperature of about 85° F in summer, feeds the Gulf Stream by the ebb and flow of the 2–3ft tide on the banks. Every second some 25 million tons of water pass at about a speed of four knots through the Florida straits. Despite the direction of the prevailing wind which is predominantly easterly, the current is actually helped on its way northwards by the Coriolis force which, because of the rotation of the earth, affects moving particles by deflecting them to the right (in the northern hemisphere) proportional to the speed of their movement. It is this phenomenon which turns the prevailing wind into a north-acting force upon the current and causes the Gulf Stream to 'race' at an almost unprecedented speed through the channel. Since the force must, according to physics, be balanced by an equal and opposite force, the water tends to 'pile' on the west side of the current which, in the case of the Gulf Stream, can cause a height difference of up to three feet between one side of the channel and the other. The Northwest Providence Channel acts as a tributary of the Gulf Stream, and inspection of the map shows how this current has greatly affected the shape of Grand Bahama by eroding the western estuary end of the island. This is where the channel meets the main body of the same Gulf Stream which has such a benign climatic effect on the islands and continent of northern Europe.

WATER RESOURCES

The island has no natural surface drainage with rivers and streams carrying the run-off down to the sea. Instead all rainfall percolates into the ground or, after severe rainstorms, the rain water sometimes forms giant puddles in developed areas where the natural 'pores' of the rock have been sealed. Sea water permeates the underground caverns in limestone below about fifty feet causing the tide to ebb and flow in any hole drilled into the ground water. Because fresh water is slightly lighter than sea water it will 'float' on the more saline water below.

The mechanics of the fresh water to sea water balance has been explained by the Ghyben–Herzberg principle. This principle states theoretically that for every foot of fresh water above mean sea level there are between 30 and 50ft of fresh water below mean sea level. The fresh water level is generally higher, therefore, in the centre of the island tapering towards both shores forming, in cross section, a convex lens. Calculations have shown that within the middle third of the island alone (making allowance for the infiltration of sea water through the cutting of canals) at least 250,000 people could be supported with potable water, assuming consumption at 100gal per person per day. The island as a whole possibly has reserves to support twice that number.

Studies indicate that about fifty-six plants in the Bahamas are indigenous though almost none of them bear edible fruit. The other species that are common to the islands have been carried by wind, ocean currents, migratory birds, or, more recently, have been imported by man. Until the middle of the twentieth century the vegetation of the island was little affected by flora introduced by man. Though most houses planted fruit trees, especially citrus, mango and banana, little imported vegetation grew wild. The great exception is the introduction of the Australian pine *(Casuarina equistifolia)* which was certainly introduced by man into the more populated islands of the Bahamas, though in the case of Grand Bahama it may have been seeded by migratory birds. At all events the casuarina was planted by the early settlers as a windbreak though its large surface root system and pine needle blanket made cultivation under or near the trees almost impossible. Today an isolated clump of casuarinas on the south shore invariably marks the site of former habitation.

The flora of the Bahamas has been recorded and codified by a number of people. As early as 1731 the colonial naturalist Mark Catesby wrote a book entitled *Natural History of the Carolinas, Florida and the Bahamas,* and around the turn of the last century several North Americans, including Agassiz of Harvard University and a geographical Society of Baltimore team headed by G. B. Shattuck, made valuable contributions to the study of

30

the plant life of the islands. The most comprehensive report made of the flora of the islands was made by Millspaugh and Britton prior to 1920 called simply *The Bahama Flora*. In 1969 a nature centre, built as a memorial to James Rand, was established in Freeport under the direction of Dr Robert Fluck where research is being carried out on the flora and fauna of the island which should greatly help to up-date the earlier studies.

The plant life of Grand Bahama is a curious mixture of northern and subtropical vegetation, more closely akin to Cuba than Florida. Such diverse forms of plant life as cacti, pines, orchids and palms thrive on the island. Except for the vegetation of the rich loamy areas and swamp land, the Bahama pine *(Pinus caribaea)* forms the most significant vegetation. This pine, which is found principally on Andros, Abaco and Grand Bahama, grows to an average height of about fifty to sixty feet and is characterised by a straight trunk, few limbs and a small topping out of branches and needles.

Forest fires play an important part in preserving the delicate balance of plant ecology on the island. Regularly, in the drought season, usually early summer, forest fires rage through the pine barren killing the underbrush and saplings. Because of their height, the mature pines generally withstand the holocaust and, with less competition, survive. The wisdom of restricting the cutting of trees of small girth can be appreciated by the manner in which the pine forest has repropagated itself. The poverty of the soil and the long periods of drought which the island sustains in the early part of the year results in the xerophytic character of the plant life. The island is sadly lacking in the indigenous, lush, tropical vegetation associated with other islands in the Caribbean.

Sapodilla (the chewing gum tree), casuarinas, cocoa plum, silver thatch palms (a source of 'straw' for basket work) and small specimens of mahogany are found generally near the south shore, and stunted thatch palms, lysilona (often mistakenly called a tamarind), tabeuia, poison wood (*Metopium toxiferum*) and low ground cover grow mostly on the Bahama stoney loam below the canopy of pines. Perhaps the most important plant, from the botanical

31

point of view, is *Psilotum nudum* or the whisk broom fern which is believed to be the world's first plant to stand upright. Known through fossils to exist 300 million years ago, it was thought by Darwin and other nineteenth-century botanists to be extinct, but it was later found to exist in the Bahamas and the West Indies in the primeval form of its ancestors.

The coral sand areas near to the south shore line have a good percentage of phosphates and potash besides a fair portion of organic matter. When cultivated they produce good crops of arrowroot (used as a starch), corn, bananas, sweet potatoes and pidgeon peas; the latter being mixed with rice to form a staple of the Bahamian diet. Growing on the dunes and helping to stabilise them one finds pioneer sea oats (*Uniola paniculata*) which grow to about four feet high and the enormously fast-growing railroad vine, a kind of morning-glory which has purple bell-shaped flowers. Inland from the dunes, sandbur and a local variety of St Augustine grass form the principal ground cover and of the shrubs, seagrape (*Caccolobis unifera*), bayberry and palmettos predominate. In the more brackish areas of the north shore and anywhere near the swash, buttonwood (*Conacarpus erecta*) and 'Ming' trees (*Bucida spinosa*) are abundant.

The present-day gardens on the island are noteworthy because of the amount of imported plant material. Though natural vegetation is sometimes retained, more one suspects for reasons of economy than ecology, it is seldom given pride of place. Generally building sites are planted with imported sodded grass, often a St Augustine type, and feature trees include imported palms, schefelera (the umbrella tree) or members of the ficus family. Shrubs include imported oleander, hibiscus, acalypha and carissa and plants might include day lilies, oyster plants and annuals. Wedelia, purple queen and springerii fern are used extensively as ground cover. About the only native plants used in gardens are the giant native cacti (*Agave caribaea*) and the silver thatch palms which are sometimes removed from swashland prior to canal development. The lack of topsoil does not make for a verdant effect in the newly developed portions of the island. Heavy engineering work, particularly in new roads and canal development, leave great limestone scars in landscape which take many years to heal and, in the case of road verges, present a very untidy appearance.

In the early days before the travelling out-island doctor service was instituted, there existed on all the islands a wealth of knowledge on the pharmaceutical properties of the native plants. Doubtless much of the 'bush medicine' can be scientifically disproved, but occasionally medical experts confirm the medical value of certain plants. Take for instance the prolific periwinkle which grows in such profusion that some consider it a weed. In the 1960s research in North America found that crystals of *Vinca* (periwinkle) caused an increase of red blood cells which proved it to be of great use in the treatment of leukemia. On Grand Bahama the leaves of the common *Tabebuia Bahamensis* (five fingers) have for a long time been used as soothing tea for 'body strain' and for the relief of backache, and the ornamental acalypha (sometimes called 'match-me-if-you-can') is reputedly good for rheumatic pains when the large leaves are crushed and applied to the affected parts. Mrs Leslie Higgs, the expert on bush medicines in the Bahamas, also notes that some believe that if it is worn in the sole of a shoe it will cure a cold! *Bidens pilosa* (shepherd's needle), a weed looking much like a daisy, is excellent for cooling 'high blood' and relieving sick stomachs and (so the remedy goes) should be given every day for nine days for worms in children; as an antidote to poison wood the juice of the leaves or bark of gum elemi (*Bursera simaruba*) should be applied to the affected skin. For 'sex weakness' *Cuscuta americana* or *Pentagona* (love vine) or *Tournetortia volubilis* (soldier vine) are the prescribed cure!

FAUNA

Islands are usually deficient in large indigenous animals and Grand Bahama is no exception. Of the present-day fauna Grand Bahama's most interesting land animal is the curly-tailed lizard, *Leicephalus carinatus armouri*. A fairly large member of the lizard family, a mature curly-tail would measure up to nearly a foot in length if his tail were unwound. There are about six distinct types of lizard on the island including the *amoles* and one *gecko*. Quite harmless the lizards can be seen everywhere sunning themselves or diving for cover into one of the ubiquitous holes of the coral rock which appear on the surface of the island.

The largest wild animal of the island is the North American racoon which grows to about two feet in length but is so shy it is seldom seen. Its diet consists of small mammals and reptiles, fruit and berries. Local folklore has it that the first racoons were brought to Grand Bahama by the bootleggers in the 1930s though it is out of the question that the racoon was such a late arrival. Also to be found in the uninhabited parts of the island are common feral cats which have reverted to a wild state.

Frogs are quite common and appear as if from nowhere after a brief shower of rain, uttering discordant, cacophonous, mating calls. The feet of the most common island frog have suckers which enable it to scale vertical surfaces. Grand Bahama also has a variety of black garter snake which grows to about two feet long. Completely harmless to humans, the garter snake kills its prey of small reptiles by crushing them in the fashion of a boa constrictor.

Insects

Though not visibly obvious the insect life of Grand Bahama has other ways of making its presence felt. A nuisance in the summer months are the mosquito, the sandfly (called 'no see 'ems' by the natives) and the horsefly. The mosquito causes itchy sores on the skin and the last two give a sharp sting which, though not generally causing sores, are a great pest. Other insects equipped with stings include ants, wild bees and scorpions. The latter are fairly small, and give a sting hardly worse than a bee. Houseflies, grasshoppers, spiders and cockroaches are also fairly common and make it imperative that buildings be equipped with fly screens. The island also possesses insects which are not an annoyance like the crickets—which provide a pleasant background sound, adding to the ambiance of the subtropical night. Also, there are

Page 35 Old and new hotels: *(above)* Star Hotel, West End, the oldest on the island; *(below)* Grand Bahama Hotel, showing swimming pool with Butlins holiday village dining-room in background

Page 36 The deluxe 265-room Lucayan Beach Hotel, opened in 1964

twenty-four varieties of butterfly in the Bahamas, some of which are migratory. The beautiful brown and white mottled Monarch (*Anonsia plexippus*), for instance, has about a three inch wing spread and travels from the north part of the continent to the Southern United States and sometimes even visits the islands. Several small species of spider help to keep the flying insect population in check. And at night moths, the nocturnal counterpart of the butterfly, almost exceed the butterfly in size and the subtlety of their markings.

Birds

The Bahama Islands have over 200 species and sub-species of birds, more than half of which are migratory and do not breed in the Bahamas. The bird life includes humming-birds, thrushes, finches, warblers, cuckoos, woodpeckers, owls, hawks and vultures; and of the sea birds, plovers, sandpipers, tropic birds, cormorants, gulls and terns are the principal species. Most of the breeding species of birds in the Bahamas are found on Grand Bahama and there are records that even the flamingo once inhabited the muddy creeks of the island. On occasion a frigate or man-of-war bird may be seen gliding over the island at a great height (pilots claim to have encountered them at 8,000ft) and sometimes heron, pelican and egret can be observed along the shore line. Generally more inland one finds the carrion-eating vulture sometimes erroneously referred to as a 'carrion crow' and sometimes called a 'turkey buzzard' by the natives on account of the similarity in appearance of the bird with a turkey when it is on the ground. When the vulture flies, however, it clearly displays a grace of flying more often associated with the eagles.

Dr James Bond and the Florida Audubon Society have prepared a list of the birds to be found in the Bahamas. The principal species which may be observed on Grand Bahama (which is on an important migration route between North and South America) include: Reddish Egret, Snowy Egret, Spotted Sandpiper, Wilson's Plover, Ground Dove, Yellow-Bellied Sapsucker, Night Hawk, Loggerhead, King Bird, Catbird, Red-legged

Thrush, Mockingbird, Black-faced Grassquits (the most common bird in the Bahamas), Brown-Headed Nuthatch, Bahama Swallow, Olive-Capped Warbler, Bahama Honey Creeper, Antillean Bullfinch and the Palm Warbler (a migrant whose summer home is in the Canadian Rocky Mountains). Warblers comprise the largest single family of birds in the Bahamas, but of the thirty-five species recorded, only a few remain in summer. The bird population has remained constant despite the influx of people. One faithful seasonal visitor to the island who 'discovered' the island long before human kind, and is still a regular visitor, is the rare species of Kirtland's Warbler (of which less than 1,000 remain), which migrates from Michigan on the North American continent to weather out the winter in the Bahamas.

Fish

It is the sea, however, that most captures the interest, for although the island is generally flat and monotonous, below the lambent turquoise surface is a wonderland. Many interesting forms of coral are found, one of which is the delicate *Gorgonia* (containing a calcareous axis and looking like filigree work). Others are formed of innumerable polyps in calcareous cups like the aptly named brain coral and the white and orange 'stag horn' coral; which so resembles the fancy headdress of a bull moose. Another form is the beautiful plant-like purple or yellow sea fans which grow to about three feet high and add their almost unreal colours to the inshore waters. Coral is important to the terrestrial growth of the island since colonies of numerous species over the centuries built up calcareous ridges or mounds which are known as coral reefs. Grand Bahama has a fringe reef lying off the southern coast part of which is exposed in places during neap tides. It is this reef which is often credited with keeping the large predatory fish away from the bathing beaches as well as breaking up the oceanic swell. Even dead coral which becomes detached supplements the marine debris and aids in silting inshore waters or building-up beaches.

The Bahamas have great numbers of molluscs in the waters

around the islands of which the bivalve and gastropod (sea snail) species predominate. Chitons can be found often clinging to the underside of rocks where they feed on small algae. But though a few can be seen on the rocky headlands of the south coast, the chiton normally prefers the cooler water of the Atlantic Ocean.

Of the gastropods the Conch or *Strombus gigas* is found in great numbers on the Little Bahama Bank. It is difficult to explain the flavour of the conch for those who have not tasted it, but suffice to say it is not unlike leathery oyster meat. At all events it is so important to the Bahamas that its exportation is prohibited. The Bahamian varieties of conch are amongst the largest univalve shellfish in the oceans. Most conchs feed on algae though some of the closely related varieties of Helmet Shells (*Cassis tuberosa, -madagascariensis, -flammea*) are carniverous and inedible. The variable colours of the inside of the shells make them especially suitable for making into cameos or merely preserving intact as ornaments. In addition to the foregoing, amateur conchologists might discover Apple Murex, Measled Cowrie, Decussate Bittersweet and West Indian fighting conch shells scattered on the beaches.

The Echinodern family is well represented in the waters of Grand Bahama and starfish (including Brittle Stars), Sea Urchins, Sea Cucumbers and Crinoids are found all around the island. In particular the exoskeletal form of the Sand Dollar (or Sea Biscuit) is found everywhere washed up on the beaches and are collected as souvenirs.

Squid and octopus are common too, though the squid normally prefers deeper water and so is not encountered so frequently as the octopus. Both animals protect themselves by emitting an inky fluid and hiding from their enemies in the smoke screen. In the Bahamas the octopus seldom grows tentacles above a foot long and it lives almost exclusively on the small fish and crabs it enmeshes in its tentacles. The octopus lives in holes in the reef or the sea bed and moves along the bottom using its tentacles as legs or it swims backwards ejecting a jet stream of water like the squid family. The octopus reproduces by laying eggs in jellied clusters on the rocks from which the young emerge as miniature adults.

Of the crab family the diminutive Sand or Ghost Crab can be seen just before its disappearing act on most of the beaches. Also seen generally in more rocky parts of the shoreline is the blue crab, which has brightly coloured blue claws. The blue crab, which grows to about 6in girth in Grand Bahama, can swim very rapidly on account of its hindmost pair of legs which are flattened and adapted for swimming. The strangest amphibious creature found along the shore is the hermit or soldier crab. This strange crustacean, as its name suggests, 'camps out' in discarded shells and, as it is in the continual process of growing, it is seen constantly pulling itself along the beach in search of a more commodious shelter. A mature hermit crab will utilise all but the largest conch shells.

Another crustacean of great importance to the Bahamas is the crawfish or clawless spiny lobster, properly known as *Panulirus argus*. Mating occurs between February and April and shortly thereafter the female lays a cluster of up to 500,000 bright orange-coloured eggs. The larvae, known as phyllosomes, swim and drift in the surface layers of the sea for a number of weeks and finally emerge as perfect crawfish about an inch long which settle into the sea bed to grow into adults. At maturity, or at least when over 1lb in weight, the crawfish may be caught by Hawaiian spear (rubber or gas-powered spear guns are prohibited in the Bahamas). Crawfish are easily spotted by their large antennae which they leave projecting from their habitat under ledges or in holes in isolated rocks. Crawfish are one of the principal commodity exports of the Bahamas.

Before the advent of tourism the Bahamas was, for a time, known for its sponges. The banks provide an ideal habitat for this lowly form of sea animal and the principal export industry of the Bahamas was built around this marine product until it was killed by disease. Today the sponge has reappeared though the natural variety have been replaced by artificial sponges in popularity. The principal commercial varieties of sponge formerly included the common bath sponges (*Hippiospongia lachne, H. canaliculata* and *H. equinoformis*).

Fish of myriad hues and shapes can be seen in the crystal-clear water around the island which includes such sport fish as the bonefish (which pound for pound is one of the gamest fish in the sea), bonito, turbot and tuna, wahoo and occasionally whales. Inhabiting the inshore waters are several species of the ray family which include the sting ray, the leopard ray (so called on account of its brown spotted markings) and the manta or devil ray. The manta is not uncommon in Bahamian waters and occasionally attains a width of 20ft across and a weight of over 2,000lb. It has a long whip-like tail, though it is not equipped with a stinging mechanism. Its main defence seems to be its sheer size and its habit of half-burying itself in the sand when at rest.

Grunts, sergeant-majors and hinds dodge in and out of the rocks of the inshore waters and very occasionally a turtle will break the surface gasping for air. The Hawksbill turtle (*Eretmo-chelys imbricata*), which can weigh as much as 200lb, is commercially the most valuable of all turtles on account of its shell, though it has rarely been seen in recent years.

The reef abounds in fish like snapper, grouper and the occasional shark. Obeying the territorial imperative the barracuda is often observed defending an area of ocean demarcated by some imaginary fence of its own making. The barracuda is a predatory fish and though exceptionally fast and equipped with a vicious set of teeth it has very seldom been guilty of an attack on a human being. Not long ago the world's record barracuda (over 103lb) was caught off the western end of the island. Further out to sea, in the deep water, abundant sail-fish, tuna and marlin make the waters off Grand Bahama among the best sport fishing grounds in the world. Unfortunately, from the commercial point of view, fishing in the Bahamas favours the line fisherman and because of this the Bahamians (who rely on fishing for their livelihood) have severe competition from the sport fisherman whose boat is often equipped with all the latest fishing devices including sonar.

GRAND BAHAMA

On the Little Bahama Bank to the north of the island, conch, bonefish and crawfish abound, and on occasion that strange amorphous mammal, the manatee or sea cow, has been observed. Schools of porpoise frequently patrol the inshore waters to the delight of bathers who take their presence as a sign that predator fish are at bay.

3   DISCOVERY AND OBLIVION

INDIAN OCCUPATION

THE first inhabitants of Grand Bahama were the primitive Siboney Indians who arrived in the northern Bahamas by island-hopping by canoe from the other islands and the Florida peninsula. Later they were overrun by the Lucayan Indians and disappeared completely. Certainly it was the Lucayans that Columbus met on arriving in San Salvador in 1492. Though he noted that the natives called themselves *Ceboynas*, which is close enough to 'Siboney' to have caused later confusion as to whether there were two indigenous peoples in the islands or only one. In their own tongue they also referred to themselves as *lukku-cairi* (island people) from which we derive the name 'Lucaya'. The people he met, he explained in his records, lived in utter simplicity, scratching an existence from primitive agriculture and supplementing their diet with food from the sea. Nevertheless he recorded that they were 'quick to learn, unwarlike, open-hearted, generous, easily won having neither religion nor idolatry, hospitable, ingenious and excellent navigators'. Peter Martyr, the author of *De Orbe Novo* written in 1511, one of the first books to be published on the 'new world', was at pains to stress that the '. . . Taini . . . were . . . noble men and not canibals . . .' (unlike their warlike neighbours the Caribs). The Lucayans were descendants of the race anthropologists classify as Arawaks. They are believed to have come from the eastern slopes of the Andes in South America, from whence they made their way to what is today Venezuela and the Guianas. From there they took to the sea and colonised the entire Caribbean including the Florida

43

Keys. There were four sub-groups of Arawak Indians : the Lucay-ans (Lucayos) of the Bahama Islands, the Taino Indians of the Lesser Antilles, the Igneri who previously had lived in the Lesser Antilles but who are thought to have been decimated by the Caribs by the time Columbus arrived, and the Trinidadian and Guianian Arawaks.

Shortly after Columbus established the first Spanish settlement at Santo Domingo he discovered his error in assuming the Indians were without religious belief and consequently commissioned one Friar Pane to make a study of their religion. The friar's account reveals that the Taino, who were the cousins of the more primitive Lucayan Indians, had a very high development of belief and ritual which later authors have suggested may be attributed to the influence of the Mayan civilisation of Central America. In Taino culture the Arawaks worshipped idols called *Zemis* or *Zemes*. The Arawaks believed these spirits lived in sacred trees and their graven images represented them as both human and animal figures in both wood and stone carvings. The Lucayans were almost as much at home in the sea as on land and they are reputed to have been seen swimming a mile or more from the shore. They are also known to have constructed canoes which could carry between 40 and 45 men. The Indians adorned them-selves by painting their bodies different colours and tying boards to the foreheads of their infants to toughen their skull bones as a defence against enemy blows—some would suggest that it was also supposed to serve the purpose of making them look more at-tractive. Arawak men wore a breech cloth and the women an apron of cotton or palm fibres, the length of which was a sign of rank. In the Bahamas, Columbus reported that the natives were quite naked (which presumably says something for their state of cultural development and social status) though they sometimes wore orna-ments made of beads, shells and occasionally gold, some of which have been found on the southern Bahama Islands. Sven Loven, the authority on Taino culture, states that shell axes are the only weapons to have been found in the Bahama Islands. The principal artifacts of note, however, were wooden ceremonial stools or *duhos* used by the tribal leaders, a few of which have been discovered in the Bahamas.

It was upon the advice of the Lucayans that Columbus sailed southwest from San Salvador to Hispaniola in search of the gold he had seen in the Bahamas and which, ironically, caused the later enslavement of the Indians at the hands of the rapacious conquistadores. However, the unfortunate Lucayans were doomed to destruction even before the coming of the white man. By the time of Columbus's landfall, war-like Caribs were invading the island of Hispaniola and would almost have certainly overrun the mild Lucayans had not the Spaniards intervened.

PONCE DE LEÓN

In 1513 three ships visited the northern islands of the Bahamas. In command of the expedition was Ponce de León, the newly appointed Governor of Puerto Rico who had a Capitulation (or concession) signed by King Ferdinand of Spain to search for the island of Bimini and the fabled *Fountain of Youth*. On 18 July the ship's log recorded that they anchored at a small island where they took on water and there met an old Indian woman. They called the island *la Vieja* after the old woman and stated their position as 'in the 28°'. If their navigator was correct, the 28° parallel would position them in the shoals of the Little Bahama Bank north of what is now West End, though they possibly might have been further south than they thought at the islet which tradition appropriately makes us call today 'Indian Cay'. It seems likely, however, that if Ponce de León landed on the cay he took on water from the mainland, a mere quarter of a mile away, and did not record this fact in his log since it would have seemed to have been of little consequence at the time. We will never know for sure what a solitary old woman was doing on the cay alone, but it is very possible that she was one of the last people left on Grand Bahama by other Spaniards who had but recently depleted the island of Indians. From *la Vieja* Ponce de León continued his search for the *Fountain of Youth* in the shallows off the north

45

of the island. He crossed from the deep water of the Channel onto the bank between Sandy Cay and Memory Rock *c*. 6 July. But since the water was shallow (about 2–3 fathoms) he sent the brigantine ahead to search for a passage for the two larger vessels. Whilst on the bank they were greatly surprised to encounter Diego Miruelo who was in the service of Diego Columbus, the brother of Christopher Columbus. Miruelo was exploring the northern Bahamas doubtless also hopeful of finding the elusive fountain. After this chance meeting Miruelo stayed with de León and was later shipwrecked in a hurricane but was saved with all hands. On the Little Bahama Bank de León's only observation was that some of the islands appeared 'to be overflowed'—an interesting description of a typical mangrove-covered sand pit. According to the account of the Spanish historian Herrera of the voyage 'they went out from the islets . . . and found it to be "bahama" '. Thus Ponce de León referred to the bank as *baja mar*, Spanish for underwater or shallow, but by the time of the publication of the Turin map in 1523 it denoted the island as well, and later it of course became applied to the entire archipelago. On 6 August Ponce de León returned to *la Vieja* suggesting that the island had good mooring, the promise of more water and perhaps a more informative interview with the old woman. It is doubtful that they met the old woman again but we can be fairly certain that they took on water because from here they set sail for Puerto Rico never to return again. Ponce de León had not discovered the *Fountain of Youth*, but perhaps, more important, he had discovered a mainland peninsula which he called Florida (for *Pascua Florida*, the Easter Day of Flowers or Easter Sunday). Ponce de León left two navigators behind him in the northern Bahamas to continue the search for the illusive fountain. These two men, Alaminos and Ortubia, were possibly the first white men to explore the interior of Grand Bahama and they doubtless took note of any Lucayans remaining on the island and reported the matter back to their Spanish master. Some months later the navigators returned to Puerto Rico but as the historian Michael Craton notes in his *History of the Bahamas*, even though they reported finding Bimini, the legendary island and 'fountain of perpetual youth', they must have glossed over the paucity of their discovery.

In 1519, Alaminos, by this time quite familiar with Bahamian waters, theorised that a return route to Spain could be followed by going north of Grand Bahama and turning east and he had a chance to prove his theory while sailing under Cortés shortly before the conquest of the Aztec Empire of Mexico. Thus the Bahama Passage became an extension of the 'Spanish Main' and the route quickly became popular with the Spanish colonists who now saw no point in settling in the Bahama Islands since there were known to be richer lands for the adventurous to the west and already established communities for the gregarious to the south. The island ceased to be of interest to the Spaniards.

Next came a period in which the island descends into oblivion. The Lucayan Indians that Columbus met on his first visit to the New World were described as a mild and gentle people dwelling in a peaceful simplicity and making a living from the sea, not so different from many present-day Bahamians. However, after 1494 when the Treaty of Tordesillas fixed the demarcation line between the overseas possessions of Spain and Portugal, the Bahamas were declared to be the domain of the Spaniards. The new European colonists had a great need for labour to work in the fisheries, mines and plantations in Hispaniola, Cuba and elsewhere and so they scoured the islands for Indian slaves. The misanthropic authorisation for the enslavement of the Lucayans was contained in a report to the king in 1508 recorded by Herrera : 'the *Lucaya* islands being full of people, it would be convenient to carry [them] over to Hispaniola, that they might be instructed in the Christon Religion, and civiliz'd . . . .' The result of this hypocritical pronouncement was seen in 1509 when Governor Ovando of Hispaniola abducted almost all the Indians from the islands to become virtual slaves of the Spaniards. The Indians had been easy to deceive since they thought they would meet their ancestors at the end of their voyage to the south—their traditional home. It is a sad matter of record that most of them died through a combination of overwork and lack of immunity to European diseases. Probably by the time Ponce de León visited the island, and certainly by the middle of the sixteenth century, the islands were de-populated and were to remain so until the coming of the English. The chronicle of the Spanish Bishop Bartoleme de las Casas, *Historia de las Indias* (first published in Spain and later in 1656 in English under the title *The Tears of the Indians*), related that after cruising the Bahamas for remaining survivors of the Lucayans he found only eleven Indians out of a population once estimated at 40,000!

EARLY MAPS

For background information on the Bahama Islands in the period that follows, the European maps of the next three centuries are a useful source. It is important to understand that in the time of Ferdinand and Isabella, maps of the newly chartered lands were a closely guarded secret. So when captains returned from their voyages the Crown made every effort to obtain both originals and copies of maps made during the voyage. Of course this secrecy increased the demand for further copies of the maps and a lucrative black-market trade often ensued. Certainly an incidental purpose of the voyage of Columbus was to gain more material for the map-making business.

The earliest map of the Americas was probably made by Juan de la Cosa in 1500, the pilot of Columbus on his second voyage (this la Cosa is not to be confused with the man of the same name who owned the *Santa Maria*). On la Cosa's map Hispaniola, Cuba and some islands to the north are shown, the northwest Atlantic Ocean is noted as *mar descubierta por yngleses* ('the sea discovered by the English') and a vague coastline of North and South America is shown. S. E. Morison, in his scholarly *Admiral of the Ocean Sea*, points out that the Bahamas on Juan de la Cosa's map are so inaccurately placed as to indicate that the cartographer had never seen them.

Martin Waldseemüller's map seven years later named the

newly discovered continent of America for Amerigo Vespucci the Florentine explorer. On the map he published he shows an archipelago of small islands north of Cuba representing the Bahamas and a peninsula which suggests the outline shape of Florida protruding from the territorial mass of North America designated, with an honest confession of ignorance, as *terra incognita* ('unexplored land'). On neither map, however, is there shown an island of similar location or shape which clearly resembles Grand Bahama, suggesting that the island had still not been explored by this date.

On the Turin map of 1523 for the first time the name 'Bahama' appears. An island the shape of Grand Bahama, however, is still indiscernible. Following the Turin map the explorer Giralamo de Verrazano drew a 'World Map' in 1529 positioning Grand Bahama correctly, but grossly overestimated the size of the island of Andros. And the same year Diego Ribero published a map and identified an island 'Bahama' and got the shape almost right, but fell in the opposite error of underestimating the size of Andros. In 1584 Ortelius showed an island 'Bahama' to the west of, and very much smaller than, Abaco (which he called Lucayonoque), so clearly no one had charted the shallows between Abaco and Grand Bahama—hence the confusion in the relative size of the islands.

The northern Bahamas by the eighteenth century had been fairly well mapped and the Little Bahama Bank had clearly been explored and was duly recorded by Guillaume Delisle in his *Carte du Mexique et de la Floride*. In 1709 a geographer, Herman Moll, produced a map of the West Indies including Central America and the Bahamas on which the island, in common with the earlier maps, is called 'Bahama', and north of West End 'Sele Key' and 'Membre Rock' are shown. All along the south of the island 'Roade Rocks' are noted somewhat indiscriminately by an *X*, the shallows to the north are called 'Bahama Banck' and the channel between the island and Florida is significantly identified as 'the best passage in all the islands'. Moll's map is interesting since the island for the first time clearly resembles the shape we

49

know today. The credit for naming the island, however, goes to the Spaniard, Antonio de Arredondo, who, on the chart he published in 1742, called the island 'Gran Bahama' (sic); though it was only early in the twentieth century before the name of Grand Bahama was the universally applied name for the island.

ENGLISH EXPLORERS

The first English ship to sight Grand Bahama was probably captained by Sebastian Cabot who explored the Land of Cod (Cape Cod, New England) and was thought by Francis Bacon to have been 'the first to come to the region of the Indies' since it is recorded that in 1519 an English warship of 250 tons arrived in Puerto Rico. The ship had followed the North American coast southwards to Puerto Rico and from San Juan the ship went on to Hispaniola where the crew bartered tin in the port of San Sebastian. As a contemporary report put it : 'the incident caused much speculation because up to that time no English warship had ever reached those islands'.

Some eight years after Cabot's voyage another English ship, the *Mary Guildford*, captained by John Rut, sailed down the North American coast bound on another illicit trading mission with the Spanish colonies to the south. Rut was followed by John Hawkins who, after three trading voyages to the Caribbean in the mid-sixteenth century, was quite familiar with the northern Bahamas, for he mentions in the log of his voyage of 1567 : the '. . . channel and gulfe of Bahama which is between the Cape of Florida and the Islands of Lucayo'. It was shortly after these English navigators had opened the way to the Indies that England, under Elizabeth I, started to consider the establishment of colonies which would serve as outposts against the growing hostility of the Spanish Empire. In 1578 Sir Humphrey Gilbert was granted the right to settle any land not already colonised in North America including, we must presume, the Bahama Islands. Afterwards Raleigh, on the recommendation of the two advisers he had sent to the New World,

50

founded the settlement of Virginia and shortly thereafter an English fleet of seven ships sailed through the Bahamas under the command of Sir Richard Grenville. Their destination was Roanoke Island but it is ironic to note that the Spaniards, on seeing the fleet off Portugal, thought that Grenville's mission was to colonise Florida or perhaps Andros or Grand Bahama Island. A contemporary observer, Don Alvaro de Baran, wrote : 'of their intentions nothing is known except that they expect more ships and appear to intend to settle. It is presumed that they will go to Florida or an island 30 leagues long which lies in the Bahamas . . . [Channel] . . . by which the fleet must sail.' Don Alvaro was clearly aware of the danger of the intended English colonisation in his allusion to the Florida Channel through which many of the laden Spanish treasure ships sailed home. The English, however, finally settled in Jamestown, Virginia, in 1607, where the first slave ship, carrying a cargo of black Africans, arrived shortly thereafter, marking the beginning of the African slave trade in North America. New England was settled thirteen years later in 1620, so with no naval base in the region of the Indies it was left to itinerant English privateers to compete with Spain for control of the Florida Channel.

Another English seadog who must have been familiar with Bahamian waters was Sir Francis Drake, whose records show that he anchored off Bimini in 1586. It was possibly as a result of his voyages that some of the first English maps of the region were published by John White. Shortly thereafter Thomas Hood, on a map printed in 1592, records an island 'Bahama' and, since the shape is more accurate than previous maps, it suggests that coastal explorations had been made (though much of the other information was almost certainly copied from earlier European maps).

Without question there was human settlement on the island from time to time. Firstly, there was possibly a residual Indian population who, too infirm or too old to work like *la Vieja*, may have been left on the island since they had no commercial value to the Spaniards. Then occasionally the reef fishermen from the

51

neighbouring islands may have spent the night by a camp fire on one of the beaches. In 1625 some French attempted to settle Abaco and though they vanished shortly afterwards they almost certainly would have been very familiar with the eastern parts of Grand Bahama. A relief ship was sent out from France but nothing is known of what became of the French settlement. Certainly the French were active in the region since there are records of a French colony being founded north of what is today Jacksonville on Fort George Island about this time. As a matter of record, in 1629 England laid claim to the Bahamas. Charles I granted all land between the latitudes of 31° and 36° north of the American mainland and the Bahama Islands to Sir Robert Heath, the Attorney General of England. The grant read (in part): '. . . and also all those our islands of beagus Bahama and all other Isles and Islands lying southerly there . . .'. Because of a drafting error 'beagus' was not capitalised. This is the island sometimes also referred to as 'Veajus' which is possibly a corruption of *la Vieja*, and, since the grant certainly refers to a northern island, it seems fair to deduce that it refers in this instance to Abaco. It is interesting to note that Grand Bahama (Bahama), too, was singled out for special reference.

PIRATES

The strategic location of Grand Bahama was not overlooked by pirates and the western tip of the island certainly saw many a ship flying the skull and crossbones and lying in wait for the merchant shipping in the Florida Channel—the 'Golden Road' back to Spain. The channel was particularly favoured since the constant current of 4 knots carried the ships northwards without complete dependence on the winds to where the westerlies begin. However, to avoid the bars of the Carolinas, some convoys turned eastward at Great Isaac Rock north of Bimini and sailed directly to the deep waters of the Atlantic between the islands of Eleuthera and Abaco. They travelled in convoy for safety and all lights were doused by night to escape attention of privateers who

52

Page 53 Relaxation and sport: *(above)* restaurant, Taino Beach, Lucaya; *(below)* typical golf course at Freeport, showing artificial lake and pine forest beyond

Page 54 (above) Moorish-style El Casino at night; *(below)* 14,000-ton MV *Freeport* which operates as ferry from mainland with night accommodation

swarmed the northern Bahamas. Needless to say the channels are littered with wrecks of ships which never made the passage to the open Atlantic.

A year before England made official claim to the Bahama Islands a maurauding Dutch privateer, Piet Heyn, surprised a Spanish fleet in Matanza Bay, Cuba, and carried away several treasure ships as a prize. Due perhaps to the lack of sufficient crew to man the additional vessels, or possibly due to more sinister reasons, two of the prize ships vanished completely with their treasure in a storm when the privateer and his convoy were in the vicinity of the northern Bahamas. Despite the loss of two ships, on arrival in the Netherlands the Great Victory of Matanza Bay was commemorated by the striking of medals depicting the audacious seaman. It is recorded that Heyn's personal bounty amounted to £700,000 and this was but a tenth of the total captured. The Spanish authorities were understandably furious at their loss and they executed the captain general and banished the admiral of the Indies fleet to North Africa.

In March 1682/3 Thomas Paine in the *Pearle*, a ship of eight guns and sixty men, received a commission from Sir Thomas Lynch (then Governor of Jamaica) to take pirates 'at the island of Bahama which is desert and uninhabited'. At Grand Bahama (probably where West End is today) he met several other ships' captains who were considering the right time to dive for silver 'out of a Spanish wreck which lies about 14 leagues from the island'. It seems that Paine forgot his original mission and entered with them into what a contemporary report called a 'confederacy'. A report from Barbados in 1683 says Paine came in a ketch from Jamaica to get pilots for the wreck 'without the limits of Bahama Island'. But news reaching Boston suggested the hope of finding much treasure was not favourable. Peres Savage had worked with six boats at the wreck 'with 30 of the best divers available and 6 good drudges [dredges] but had shared but 7½lbs of plate [silver] a man . . . he left six sails there but considered their prospects poor'. Presumably because the salvage operations at Grand Bahama were going so badly Paine and the other ships' captains later sailed under false colours and sacked some settlements around St Augustine in Florida.

There are public records of a great deal of salvaging and pirate activity at Grand Bahama soon after the first English settlement was made in Eleuthera. In 1684–5 a map was made for a Captain Phips which shows Membre (Memory) Rock and the location of three wrecks. Though Phips was doubtful that there was much silver left after Captains Cornway and Wooley had fished 'for pigs and sows of silver' and had retrieved but '14 lugs from that island'. However, soon afterwards in 1687 Phips made his historic find of treasure, after three years' search, at the area in the southern Bahamas now known as Silver Banks. After a salvaging operation lasting twelve weeks Phips and his crew salvaged 12 tons of gold and other precious metals from a wreck!

Only a few of the many treasure ships sunk in Bahamian waters have been discovered. Several years ago Mr Howard Lightbourn and Mr Roscoe Thompson, Nassauvian businessmen, made an important find off Gorda Cay, an islet off the southeastern tip of Grand Bahama, from which wreck a 70lb silver bar and many Spanish coins were found. The silver bar has been identified by experts as a Guanajuato type since the boat shape of the ingot was first adopted by the mining centre of that name in Mexico. Despite the ingot type however, the assayer's mark suggests that the silver originated in the Kingdom of New Granada or what are today the South American republics of Venezuela and Columbia. It was thought that the wreck might have been the *San Pedro* which is known to have broken away from a convoy and been sunk either by pirates or a hurricane, but the evidence is inconclusive. Certainly it is known that around the turn of the seventeenth century many treasure ships were sunk in Bahamian waters, many of which have still to be located, the more important of which include the *Golden Hind*, the *Santa Cruz*, the *El Capitan* and the *Porto Pedro*. As the most dangerous passage these ships had to negotiate was near the northern islands of the Bahamas, it is highly likely that many of the treasure ships foundered in the

56

vicinity of Grand Bahama and southern Abaco. In fact, the activities of the English pirates working from Grand Bahama, together with some residents of Nassau (which was settled around 1670), caused the sacking of the island of New Providence on two occasions by the Spanish in 1683 and 1684. It was not until after the fortifications of Forts Charlotte and Fincastle were built in 1789–92 that the threats of further Spanish attacks were minimised (though the settlements made by the Treaty of Paris, dated 3 September 1783, officially confirmed the suspension of Anglo-Spanish hostilities).

The infamous Edward Teach, alias 'Blackbeard', was known to have frequented the northern Bahamas, and in fact the natives of Water Cay claim that a pirate of that name was captured off the northern tip of their islet, notwithstanding the fact that history records that 'Blackbeard' was captured and killed in the colony of Virginia. The story of the pirates is essentially a record of brutality and greed on the high seas, the romance of which nevertheless improves with the telling. It is the story of headstrong adventurers and of early settlers who endured dreadful hardships but who finally gave up the unequal task of making a New Jerusalem in a new world. The Crown in far-off England sanctioned 'privateers' whose only difference from pirates was that they preyed mostly on enemy shipping. Unlike the buccaneers, who were originally sedentary, pirates and privateers lived their lives aboard ship and their only visits to settlements were to victual, plunder or wench. Undoubtedly uninhabited islands like Grand Bahama served as a land base where they would occasionally hide out while awaiting their next encounter.

When Nicholas Webb became governor under the Lords Proprietors in 1696, the islands were, by his own admission, a common retreat for pirates and rogues of all kinds and were to remain so for at least another twenty-two years until Woodes Rogers became the first royal governor. Avery, Horningold, Vane, Teach and hundreds of lesser known pirates literally swarmed all over the Bahamas in search of plunder before Woodes Rogers, himself once a pirate, subdued piracy and gave the Bahamas its former motto: *Expulsis Piratis Restituta Commercia* ('pirates expelled, commerce restored').

Because of the lack of natural harbours on Grand Bahama it is unlikely that any English colonist settled there, though doubtless the Eleutheran Adventurers and the later Abaconians visited occasionally to fish and to lumber. This assumption is borne out by Governor Phenny's report of 1721 in which about fifteen islands were listed as inhabited but no mention was made of any population on Grand Bahama. Nevertheless he recorded that the island grows 'fine timber' and that the soil along the south coast is 'white land' (coral sand) known to yield 'fair crops of corn'. It was known ever since the first European discoverers of the Bahama Islands that Grand Bahama afforded abundant fresh water and the sea and creeks produced large quantities of fish and turtle, especially the Hawksbill turtle which is 'often catcht which has the fine shell so much us'd in England'.

In 1784, a German traveller, Schoepf, included Grand Bahama among a list of 'more important islands, most of them *settled in a fashion*' (italics mine). It is doubtful that there was any permanent habitation, however, since Lord Dunmore, then Governor of the Bahamas, reporting to London in 1790, made note that Grand Bahama was uninhabited 'as yet'. This last phrase does suggest that some activity was possibly imminent and, in fact, on 3 January 1792 the sale of 240 acres was recorded near the west end of the island, though there is no record of any habitation at this time. David McKinnon, about ten years later near the western tip, was able to observe from his shallow boat that 'there was not the least appearance of cultivation on the island but I could not behold the beautiful and fragrant woods over the white sands, without recurring to the fate of that innocent race of people whose name it bears. . .[the writer here erroneously presumes that 'Bahama' was the name of the original inhabitants of the Bahama Islands]. . . but who have long since been dragged from their native shores by the merciless ambition and avarice of the European visitors'. During this era in the Bahamas it is very possible that the occasional runaway slave may have found refuge on the island prior to the emancipation of the slaves in 1834, but if he built or cultivated anything the evidence would, of course, have been well concealed.

4   RESETTLEMENT

THE outside world affected neither island nor colony in the early nineteenth century. In the war of 1812 a small force of British men-of-war patrolled the Florida Channel to enforce the blockade of the United States. However, the island served only to mark the eastern boundary of the channel and was of no strategic importance in the war. After the hostilities the Admiralty charted the Manatilla Shoal north of the Little Bahama Bank. The American hydrographer Edmund Blunt also prepared a large-scale chart of the sea around the island in 1833, noting that there was fresh water at two anchorage points at West End and South East Point respectively, though 'West End' was mysteriously identified on the map as an island community just east of the Bight. Reference was also made to the Maternillo Bank (the spelling of this shoal is never twice the same even today) which, noted Blunt, the Spaniards believed to be, not a reef, but where 'the shock of the current from the sea from the north and west causes breakers'. An officer in the Royal Navy, DeMoyne, was later responsible for exposing this statement as a dangerous half-truth.

In 1836 the recorded population of Grand Bahama was about 370 persons and by the outbreak of the American Civil War the population had increased to 1,300. With the American Civil War the Bahamas became a staging-post for running the Union blockade to the Southern ports. Most of the Confederate shipping kept to starboard of Abaco on its run to Savannah and other Southern ports, the reason probably being that the Union ships could easily police the 65 miles of the Florida Channel between Grand Bahama and the mainland. However, not all the blockade runners took the Atlantic route, and some Southerners unquestionably used West End as a base to run ammunition and vital food supplies to the Confederate forces in Florida.

The oldest person alive in the Bahamas in 1971 was probably the Reverend Thomas Heild, MBE, JP, born in 1862 in Freetown. By his reminiscences Mr Heild has been a valuable source of information on Grand Bahama from the mid-nineteenth century to the present day. During his lifetime spent on the island he was once a police constable, a 'superintendent of the shore' and later a Baptist minister. It is possible to reconstruct, from his own account, what life in early years was like. Fishing was the main occupation of the menfolk, supplemented by agriculture in which women and men participated. The people were independent yet God-fearing and their way of life was something like the pristine Christians, since they were so poor they shared almost all material possessions in common. Their conversation was laced with homespun doxologies which persist today in such expressions as 'de Lawd will provide', 'Gawd be praised' and 'if Gawd give life'. The principal churches were Anglican and Baptist, the latter being in the stewardship of Mr Heild who, for a large portion of his life, visited every parish from More's Island to West End once every two weeks, his promethean efforts spent on behalf of the mere 148 Baptists who were recorded as being on the island in 1864.

As if the difficulties of resettlement were not enough, Governor Rawson reported that same year to London that Grand Bahama was an extensive island which had 'greatly declined in its products and general importance . . . where the soil has been sadly impoverished by the injurious burning of the land' and which 'was not convenient or safe for protracted visits by the police magistrate . . . on account of the boisterous sea along the south coast'. The governor reported that a gang of about forty Grand Bahamians had but recently gone to Abaco to work in preparing turpentine and tar, and yet others had migrated to Nassau and Bimini. In 1864 Grand Bahama boasted but one school and thirty-three students. The Grand Bahama Census of 1861 registered a population of 858 but in 1871 the population had diminished by more than 40 per cent from the earlier figure. The attraction of Nassau as a blockade-running port had attracted many out-islanders to the capital. It was this destitute period in the Bahamas that gave special meaning to the expression 'a shilling in Grand Bahama is worth a pound of money'.

In 1888 a barrister from England named Powles visited Grand Bahama as a guest of the school inspector. Landing most probably at what is today Eight Mile Rock he was greeted by 'an African gentleman' called Mr Adderley, who was the local magistrate and school teacher. He counted ninety-nine young children in the school and was soon in no doubt that their favourite subject was music. He remarked on the Scottish influence on the island in the names of people and places and this observation must have been further confirmed when the school children broke into song with the 'Blue Bells of Scotland'. During his stay in Eight Mile Rock, Powles walked a mile to Hawksbill Creek and on his way jotted in his notebook that he saw cows grazing, watched the natives boatbuilding, chewed some sugar cane and explained the method of local house building. In fact, one gets the general impression from his report that Eight Mile Rock was a typical out-island settlement.

CROWN GRANTS

After the Revolutionary war was over 114 grants of Crown land were made to the Loyalists from the American colonies. In total this amounted to 40,000 acres on sixteen islands, yet not a single parcel of land was granted on Grand Bahama. The reason for the omission of Grand Bahama was probably due to its lack of sheltered natural harbours, the general infertility of the soil and the time-honoured custom of ignoring the island as a useless pine barren. It was not until 1 February 1806, when one Joseph

Smith was granted 500 acres of land at the west end of the island, recorded on p96 of the first record book in the Bahamas Registry Office, that the first settlement was established. According to the deeds, this parcel of land had its northern boundary adjacent to an anchorage for shallow draught vessels and a sand beach to the south; the other identifying survey monuments of the plat require a knowledge of local trees; the northwestern boundary marker was a poison wood tree, the northeastern corner was a blackwood tree and the southeastern monument was a 'Blollywood' tree. Despite the rather vague survey description, from this date onwards we have little more recorded information about the island.

In 1812 Joseph Hunter, a member of the governor's council in Nassau, took title to 800 acres of land on the rocky coast east of Hawksbill Creek. Part of the aptly named 'eight miles of rock', this eastern tract is today occupied by the villages of Pinder's Point, Lewis Yard and Hunter's. Four years later a man named Bootle was granted 960 acres near the settlement at West End. A tract of 200 acres on what is now Lucayan Beach was granted to William Heild in 1819 and Archibald Taylor, a major in the British army, received the deeds to 60 acres of land in 1827 at what is today Russell Town just south of the developed area of Freeport. The Peterson's Cay settlement, of which only a church remains, dates from 1834 when Nathaniel Sweeting was granted from the Crown 126.39 acres in fee simple, and the land on which the Freetown settlement was located was first deeded in 1828 with subsequent grants in 1857. Three other Crown grants are interesting : the first is the grant of 320 acres to Thomas Braudie recorded in the Registry Office in Nassau in about 1830, which possibly sets the date for the establishment of Eight Mile Rock (the western portion of the 'eight miles of rocky shore'); another was a grant of 23.70 acres of land to Caroline Smith on the west side of Gold Rock Creek, which parcel, because of the small natural harbour it abutted, was very possibly the site of the original settlement at Golden Grove; and the last was a grant of 1,040 acres to one Armbrister in 1816 at Carrion Crow Harbour (now McLean's Town).

Some of the early settlers were possibly Loyalists and their slaves who, after their misfortunes on other islands, were determined to try their luck on Grand Bahama. Others probably migrated from the nearby island of Bimini. After the Emancipation Act of 1834, freed slaves settled the southern coastline; the community of Freetown, for instance, was almost certainly named for abolition of slavery in the Bahamas which antedated that of the United States by nearly thirty years. By statute the ex-slaves could purchase tracts of a minimum of twenty acres for a fixed price of 12s an acre. Many of the larger parcels of land were granted originally in the first part of the nineteenth century but after 1834 we find several grants were made to the new freemen. In 1847, for instance, there was a conveyance of 100 acres, identified by 'fig tree stakes' adjacent to the land now occupied by the Anglican church at Eight Mile Rock which records on the deed that the beneficial owner was 'Prince Clear-Free Black'. Land grants on the island prior to the recent development boom formed a patchwork quilt occupying over half of the southern shoreline, almost every parcel having at least one boundary line on the sea. The great majority of the Crown grants to private owners on Grand Bahama Island were made between the end of the first decade of the nineteenth century and the turn of the century; in some cases the grants were to servants of the Crown who never occupied the lands and in other cases to freed slaves who lived on the land with their families.

In the case of lands granted to the Bahamians who lived on the land, as most were illiterate and there was very little civil administration on the island, the records of births, marriages and deaths were usually very sketchy. Few people left wills and virtually no one bothered applying to have grants of probate or letters of administration in respect of the estates of deceased people, so the land was inhabited from generation to generation by the descendants of the original grantee. The result of this was that

64

although the law of primogeniture applied in the Bahamas and the land descended from eldest son to eldest son, as the entire family usually worked the land, various members of the family would be given little plots of land and these were regarded as their own property which they could sell or dispose of as they pleased. However, no formal documentation was ever made and consequently, except by establishing valid claims for adverse possession, most of the land, though legally belonging to only one person, was in effect occupied and possessed by several people who considered themselves the legal owners of the land.

In order to acquire this land, which comprised the bulk of the prime beach front land on Grand Bahama, it was necessary for later purchasers to buy the same piece of land in some cases from as many as ten possible owners. In addition to this, many of the private owners who sold in the post-war period in fact did not give vacant possession of the property when they signed their conveyances, and it was necessary in some cases to make quite large payments in order to induce these people to remove themselves from the land they had in fact already sold.

WRECKING

From time to time fate would render the islanders a prize in the form of a wreck (or *rack* as it is pronounced in the Bahamian dialect). Under maritime law the first people to throw a line to a foundering and abandoned ship had salvage rights over the vessel which would then be scavenged for anything of value. So well accepted and organised was this trade that 'wreckers' were licensed by the government which took one-fifth and the Crown one-tenth of the prize. In fact in the mid-nineteenth century two-fifths of all 'imports' consisted of goods saved from wrecks. To illustrate that the elements are oblivious to rank or title, Grand Bahama had an unscheduled visit by a man of God when Father Gibbons, later a famous American cardinal, was shipwrecked off the island in 1853. Though this particular mishap can be blamed on the elements, there is little doubt that misleading navigation lights and dishonest captains caused the foundering of a great number of ships.

In 1866 a serious hurricane hit the islands and a total of sixty-three ships were grounded that year, though the cause of nineteen of the wrecks was officially cited as 'mysterious'. By some reports the wreckers were accused of killing the survivors but yet others suggest the wreckers performed acts of heroism in saving passengers from drowning. A not inconsiderable part of the wreckers' reward was in 'gratitude money' from the people who were saved, though it is ironic to consider that the wreckers themselves were responsible for many of the stranded vessels. Governor Rawson noted that of the 313 wrecks in the Bahamas in 1859–64 (of which 259 were total losses), thirty-five were on the windward side of the Little Bahama Bank (thirty-one off eastern Abaco) and ten were on the leeward side, making a total of fourteen which would presumably be near to Grand Bahama Island. Of the wrecks Rawson reports 110 were British, 157 American, 13 French, 6 Spanish and the remainder were of other nationalities. It is interesting to note that thirteen of the wrecks were steamers and of those four were steam-powered men-of-war.

Bimini was a centre for wreckers whose sphere of influence included Grand Bahama and extended as far north as the Mantanilla shoal. After the Imperial Lighthouse Service built Great Isaac Light north of the Biminis in 1859 and installed other lights, the number of ships going aground was greatly reduced. However, early in the twentieth century a few ships were grounded, particularly on the shoals of the Little Bahama Bank. One was the SS *Cecilia* which was carrying a cargo of sugar from Cuba. Many of the older people on the island still remember the short-lived bonanza gained from transporting the thousands of bags of salvaged sugar to Nassau.

From the 1870s onwards Grand Bahama witnessed a rapid recovery of population which lasted until the first part of the twentieth century. This was a period of increased activity largely attributable to sponge fishing.

A map produced in 1871 by a traveller from Boston named
James Stark showed Grand Bahama as having settlements at
McLean's Town, Golden Grove, Freetown and Eight Mile Rock;
West End strangely is not recorded. The shoals at the north of
the Little Bahama Bank were shown as the 'Manilla Reef' and
the island was called Gt (for Great?) Bahama, copying presumably the nomenclature shown on the earlier English maps. It was
around the turn of the century that the Little Bahama Bank was
opened to sponge fishing. The first spongers were the Abaconian
'conchs' (white Bahamians), though later Grand Bahamians and
Greeks—who brought the industry to the Bahamas in the first
place—became involved with the trade in the northern Bahamas.
In 1902 over one million pounds of Bahamian sponge, valued at
£97,544, was exported from the colony.

A graphic picture of sponging in the Bahamas was captured in
the water colours of Winslow Homer who visited the Bahamas
in the late nineteenth century. Besides his famous painting *The
Gulf Stream* which shows a Bahamian fisherman on a demasted
Bahamian sloop surrounded by hungry sharks, Homer also
painted other Bahamian scenes including *Sponge Fisherman,
Bahamas* (collection of William P. Wadsworth), the *Sponge Diver*
and *Bahamas* (Museum of Fine Arts, Boston), all portrayed in
brilliant colours and strong contrasts, exemplifying a seascape as
seen under the Bahamian sun.

The best sponging grounds were the Andros mud flats and the
area north of More's Island at the eastern end of Grand Bahama,
appropriately called 'the Mud'. The sponge fishermen usually
owned a schooner which acted as a 'mother ship'. From this pairs
of men in dinghies would fan out while the guide sculled and the
hooker scanned the sea bottom with a glass-bottomed bucket.
When a sponge was spotted the hooker took his long-handled,
two-pronged rake, deftly hooked it from the sea bottom and
scooped it into the boat. After the dinghy was filled they returned
to the mother ship. Catches accumulated on the deck of the

schooner near a good sponging area from Sunday to Saturday, by which time the older people say the boat could be detected by scent faster than by eye. The sponge-laden schooner then sailed to a collection depot near its home island, and the sponges were left to soak in corrals or water areas fenced with sticks (the Little Bahama Bank schooners generally used Red Shank Cay). After soaking for several days in the corrals the sponges were cleaned by being tapped around with a wooden bat. At the end of eight or nine weeks the corrals were emptied and the schooner headed for the Nassau Sponge Exchange, after which the cycle was repeated year round, weather permitting. In the period from 1900 to 1905 more than a million pounds of sponge were exported each year from the colony. At its peak, sponge from the Bahamas rivalled the total production of the eight traditional sponge areas of the Mediterranean and furnished nearly 30 per cent of the world sponge harvest. Despite some overcutting in the early 1920s, sponge was to remain the principal export of the country for nearly half a century.

EARLY TWENTIETH CENTURY

One of the most authoritative sources for the history of the Bahamas up to this time was made by the Geographical Society of Baltimore in 1905, but even at this date so obscure was Grand Bahama that in over 600 pages of text the island only rates a few references and those concern shells, birds and trees found on the island. On a map that is reproduced in the book no settlements are shown and Miami on the Florida east coast, though incorporated in 1896, was of so little consequence that it too did not merit mention. Another reference to the island's natural history is found in Britton and Millspaugh's *Bahama Flora*, which notes that one L. J. K. Brace visited Eight Mile Rock in 1905, identified and collected the beautiful yellow-flowered orchid found growing in trunks and crooks of tree branches near the village. Specimens of the orchid, *Oncidium bahamense*, were taken to the herbarium of the New York Botanical Garden.

Shortly after the turn of the century an American firm, styled the Bahamas Timber Company and incorporated in 1906, obtained a concession to lumber Grand Bahama, Abaco and Andros. Not much is known of their operation on Grand Bahama though it is on record that the headquarters of the operation was in Abaco and their total annual output was about 12 million board feet most of which was exported to Cuba. In 1916 they suspended operations.

During the First World War the focus of world attention was Europe, and the Bahama Islands—never very important in the Imperial scheme—were all but forgotten. Shortly after the outbreak of war the German ship *Karlsruhe* was discovered in Bahamian waters but she was surprised by HMS *Suffolk* and slipped away to the neutral port of San Juan, Puerto Rico, and that was about all the action to be seen in the Bahamas. The colony resigned itself to quietude and Grand Bahama to oblivion. It was an exceptional day in 1917, therefore, when an English lady inquired in Nassau for a passage to a remote island in the northern Bahamas. She reports: 'I had some trouble finding it [the Grand Bahama Mail Boat] for nobody in Nassau cares two straws about Grand Bahama and [even] at the Post Office nobody knew when the boat would sail.' Eventually the boat did sail, however, with Miss Defries, the commissioner's wife, also an Englishwoman, two babies and the Bahamian passengers and crew. Miss Defries was seasick on the crossing but notes with candour that 'the gentle kindness of the coloured folk [on deck while she was sick] I shall never forget'; and, on arrival, 'the Grand Bahama people are noted for their honesty and are as clean in their extreme poverty as one can be'. There being no harbours, the mail boat had to lay off-shore and wait for the dinghies to arrive from the settlements to act as tenders. After the sickness of the voyage Miss Defries must have been quite anxious to get to dry land, however. While she was being sculled ashore at the east end of the island she had a scare when they encountered sharks in the shallow water between the boat and the shore. Though most sharks in Bahamian waters are harmless any encounter with a shark is cause for apprehension.

Whilst in Grand Bahama Miss Defries visited Eight Mile Rock shortly after the Astor's yacht reluctantly put in with a seasick guest; since there was no resident doctor in Grand Bahama the famous visitors continued their way. Had they known, they might have sent for a 'medicine woman' called Aunt Celia, who reputedly prescribed and administered the desired cure with the reassuring phrase: 'nobody never dies of my treatments'. It seems surprising her patients did not die, however, since besides using massage and herbs from the bush in her treatment she also claimed on occasion to use cow's gall and a rusty old nail! For physiotherapy Aunt Celia used tallow candles or lard; to heal wounds she boiled the traditional 'shepherd's needle'; for inflation she ordered 'pepper grass'; and for tooth decay the cure was hot cobbler's wax rubbed in daily to 'kill out de worrum what eats de teet away'. Though Miss Defries was given to understand that there was much Obeah practised on the island, Aunt Celia remonstrated that *she* believed in 'no such ting'.

Miss Defries goes on to tell a delightful story of a 'bashtad' (bedstead). On her visit to Grand Bahama she was quite captivated by the painstaking craftsmanship of a local carpenter named Josiah Anthem who had made an ornate family-sized bedstead. In fact so captivated was she that she transported the periwinkle blue, red and white bedstead all the way to Nassau on the mail boat with a view to selling it there for the local carpenter. To her annoyance the native craftsmanship was not to the sophisticated Nassauvians' liking and Miss Defries was unable to find a buyer. What happened to the 'bashtad' she does not say. It is just possible it was sent back to Grand Bahama for Josiah, the man who made it, to lie on it.

A later visitor to the island was an English Baptist minister, the Reverend J. H. Poole. In a letter to the Reverend Heild, written in 1928 and postmarked Nassau, he regretted that he had not met his fellow minister on his visit to the island but charged him to continue to look after the northern parishes from More's Island

70

Page 71 Government and business: (right) Lynden O. Pindling, prime minister in early 70s; (below left) Jack Hayward as vice-president of Grand Bahama Port Authority; (below right) James Rand, inventor, industrialist and founder of Rand Memorial Clinic

Page 72 (above) Signing of the Hawksbill Creek Agreement, August 1955. Mr Wallace Groves (left) and Rt Hon A. G. H. Gardner-Brown, acting governor of the Bahamas; (below) Central Freeport with industrial area and airport in distance

to West End. He went on to warn that John Kemp of McLean's Town 'is a seller of liquor' [according to Nemiah Thomas]. However, should Nemiah Thomas prove to be a liar 'you know just what to do with him'. We will probably never know who received the admonition.

5 INDUSTRY, BOOTLEGGING AND TOURISM

A FTER World War I Grand Bahama was destitute. In the early 1920s the total population of Grand Bahama was recorded as 1,695 persons, indicating that there had been a decrease in population since 1911 of 129 people. The colony as a whole also declined in population over the same period. There was hope of change, however, since Miss Moseley, a contemporary historian of the Bahamas, recorded that a promising new business, the Grand Bahama Mercantile and Development Company, were to launch a large scheme for the development of the island. One of the forward-looking aims of this firm was to act as a clearing house for the delivery of seafoods to the United States. Unhappily, though, the company failed with the Florida land crash of 1926 but not before they had prepared a plan showing property ownership on the island. The effort spent on preparing this plan suggests that they had some thought of land development in mind.

It was probably a representative of this same group that Major Bell, a Scottish-Canadian, met on his visit to Grand Bahama. He recalls meeting a man 'whose pockets were as full of blueprints as his head was of plans'. His confidant was obsessed by the fact that Palm Beach was only sixty miles away and liquor was cheap in Grand Bahama (a mere 30 minutes flying time from the United States) and so he was trying to promote the establishment of a casino on the island for people who, as he put it, were looking for 'real exclusiveness'. Major Bell repeats the familiar refrain that Grand Bahama had to that time been 'a sort of lost child of the colony'. He reported that travelling up Hawksbill Creek

74

among the mangroves is a picturesque adventure, but 'getting ashore thereabouts has its difficulties'. He also goes on to state, quite erroneously, that the island was only permanently settled in the 1880s though the lack of permanence about him understandably led to this false impression.

A temporary respite was ahead, however; once more events outside the colony were to affect its history. A hint of what was in store can be inferred from the number of ships in Bahamian ports during 1926. In that year 1,135 vessels entered Grand Bahama which represented the second highest number of vessels and the fourth highest tonnage entering any Bahamian port. By this time West End had been declared a port of entry and the commissioner had moved there from Eight Mile Rock and a wireless telegraph link with Nassau had been instituted.

PROHIBITION

The reason for the increase in marine traffic was that in 1919 the United States Congress had passed the Volstead (Prohibition) Act disallowing the public sale of beverages containing over half of one per cent of alcohol. Unpopular from the beginning, it was soon clear that Prohibition was contrary to the wishes of the great majority of Americans and several entrepreneurs set about making good the deficiency of liquor which ensued. The Bahamas soon became a centre for the traffic of alcoholic beverages to the United States, and home port for as many as 400 boats that ran the cordon of US Coast Guard vessels which patrolled the mainland.

The liquor reaching West End was usually transhipped via Nassau from Europe and Canada though it is recorded that at least one shipload came direct from England. Many of the centreboard sailing boats which were used for ferrying liquor from Nassau were built by Felix Bowe who owned a boatyard and was the local collector of revenue (people seldom wore just one hat in the underpaid Bahamian Civil Service at this time). In West End the liquor was stored in half a dozen or more warehouses strung out along the coastal road. Two native Grand Bahamians, Wilchcombe and Augustus 'Gussy' Hepburn, were among the first to establish warehouses, each of which had its own dock. Later they were joined by a few more Bahamians and Americans. Because of the shallow draught of about 7ft, generally small boats only were used in the trade, though occasionally shrimp boats would be employed which would carry a few thousand cases of hard liquor to ports in Georgia and the Carolinas. One ploy used by these bigger boats was to tow a cigar-shaped tube behind the boat. The 'cigar' was constructed of steel and had a capacity of over 400 cases of spirits. If a Coast Guard cutter was sighted the 'cigar' would be cut loose and the boat would change course. If the vessel was searched the Coast Guard would of course find nothing and they would be allowed to resume their journey. At night the boat would return to the site of the jettisoned liquor and, by circling the area, would locate the 'cigar' and resume its original mission.

Major Bell described the scene : after the pine barrens and primitive settlements to the east, West End was a veritable 'bright spot' where, facing the coastal road flanked with bars and warehouses, there was moored a fleet of grey, lowhulled motor-engined cruisers and some half a dozen aeroplanes. Whilst in West End he met a motley array of bootleggers including an old Cambridge graduate and an ex-RAF squadron-leader who told him, almost with nostalgia, how he had got his plane riddled with bullets in flying the blockade. The blockade runners were a lost legion of men, tough, spirited, adventuresome and certainly avaricious. The talk in the bars was of past 'scrapes' and of future plans on how to evade the 3,500 United States officials who, with 390 vessels and 5 planes, were enforcing the blockade and of the men like 'Big Nick' or 'Red' who had been 'copped', and 'sent down' for a 'stretch'. ('Red', according to Miss de Vries in her book *Fortunate Isles*, was 'Red' Shannon, a strangely miscast Robin Hood of the bootlegging brigade.) There was a tale of a bootlegger who towed a Coast Guard cutter, which was in distress, to safety within the Miami bar, only to be arrested by the men he had saved; it was reported at the time that he got sentenced to seven years in the 'pen' for his pains!

One of the bootleggers who later stayed on was Paul Mack who operated out of West End with a 48ft-long boat: the MV *Pride*. The *Pride* was powered with two 450hp Liberty engines and was capable of travelling at 40mph with a load of 400 cases of liquor. The object of the exercise was of course to avoid the US Coast Guard and with speed like this (aided by locally instituted radio interference) the bootleggers were able to land their precious cargo in pre-agreed secret rendezvous in the creeks and rivers of Florida.

Several enterprising Grand Bahamians were involved in the rum-running business using either their own boats or crewing for the Nassauvian and foreign entrepreneurs. Luther Johnson, better known as 'Duke', was on a mission at Jenson Beach, Florida, at a depot for the illicit 'booze' when armed Prohibition officers raided the premises. Professing ignorance the bootlegging West Enders almost convinced the officers until one of them suggested searching a storage shed nearby. As soon as the officers turned their backs the Bahamian bootleggers took to the woods, and after cutting palemetto leaves they jumped into a pond camouflaging their heads with the fronds. They remained like this all afternoon until the evening when they knew the Prohibition officers would be off-duty. The officers had instructions to shoot bootleggers who were attempting to escape arrest. Not everyone was as fortunate as 'Duke', however; on more than one occasion it was not United States officials who intercepted the bootleggers, but hijackers. As the bootleggers were landing their cargo the hijackers would step out of an ambush brandishing sub-machine guns and commandeer the liquor. Several bootleggers, both foreign and Bahamian, were liquidated in such hold-ups.

The United States Coast Guard were an ever-present nuisance to the bootleggers and occasionally a cutter would lie just outside the harbour, well within territorial waters though. Since they could claim that they were technically 'underway', it did not constitute a breach of international law. One day Major Bell overheard an animated conversation between a conch 'fisherman' and the crew of the cutter which we might suppose would be better grounds for litigation. In West End the bootleggers, besides building warehouses for the liquor, also constructed slips for the boats and cut an airstrip out of the bush where the present Grand Bahama Hotel is located. From here pilots in single-engined planes, dangerously overloaded with liquor, flew as many as thirty flights a day into the United States. The Reverend Heild recounted that during this period a boat carrying liquor was grounded near Mangrove Cay one Sunday. The master of the vessel wanted the reverend gentleman to haul the liquor in his skiff to West End for 'big money' but the idea conflicted with the Baptist minister's notion of temperance and Sunday observance so the offer was declined.

Big money was to be made in bootlegging and Al Capone and other infamous members of the American underground were reputed to be occasional visitors to West End. When the competition got too brisk, as in 1927 for instance, the Mobley and Ashley gangs raided West End and held up the place 'gangster style' and made off with 'loot' stolen from their competitors. Gussy Hepburn was one of the people who was tied up, gagged and robbed in the raid. By all accounts West End at this time was a den of iniquity, bars and pool rooms had sprouted up and suicides, drunken orgies and gun fights were commonplace. To keep the peace in this volatile situation the Government entrusted the maintenance of law and order to the commissioner and two policemen!

FISHING

By 1933 the Prohibition Act in the United States was replaced by the 21st Amendment and West End reverted to its former role of a sleepy out-island fishing village. Some of the people who stayed caught sharks and shipped the skins under contract to the Ocean City Leather Company in New Jersey. The shark fins had a rather more bizarre destination: they were shipped to New

York for re-shipment to China, where presumably they were consumed as a delicacy. The shallows of West End are rich in that Bahamian staple : the conch, which is made into chowders, is frittered, boiled, diced and eaten raw. Bahamians even claim the conch is an aphrodisiac and occasionally the conch renders its finders a bonus in the form of a pink pearl, one of which was recently valued at $9,000. The sea around West End also abounds with all kinds of scaled fish as well as turtle and crawfish. The latter, a clawless lobster, was caught in fairly large numbers and exported live to the east coast of Florida just prior to the outbreak of World War II. It would be difficult indeed to starve in the Bahama Islands, but the inevitable diet of seafood would become monotonous to say the least! As if to add to their miseries, in 1938 a microscopic fungoid called the 'blight' killed the sponge in the Bahamas thus ending the 40-year-old sponging industry and reducing the population even further towards subsistence.

When the war was declared in 1939 Grand Bahama had a population of just over two thousand people. The European theatre of war was far away and yet contemporary reports suggest that there was an unfeigned loyalty on the part of the Bahamians to the Allied cause. Axel Wenner-Gren, the Swedish millionaire and owner of Hog (now Paradise) Island, opened a canning factory at West End. Called General Seafood Limited, the company canned fish and Bahamian lobster as part of the war effort. The company employed many Bahamians at the plant and also maintained some ships to collect crawfish from depots on other islands as well as to engage in deep sea fishing for themselves. In 1941 the Duke of Windsor, at the time Governor of the Bahamas, visited West End to visit the factory aboard Axel Wenner-Gren's yacht *Southern Cross*. The duke's visit was evidence that he intended to get to know the Bahamas during his term as governor and the *Bahamas Handbook* records that for one old Bahamian lady it also proved his humanity for on seeing him she exclaimed, 'oh my Gawd, you mean to say he duz walk and talk and act like people? now dat's sumptin' hey?'

GRAND BAHAMA

ABACO LUMBER COMPANY

In autumn of 1944 the Abaco Lumber Company moved to Grand Bahama, having temporarily exhausted the pine lumber supply of Abaco Island. The Grand Bahamian pine is a long-leaf, yellow conifer and is a heavy wood with, as the Bahamians say, 'plenty blood' (sap) and even when properly cured it has a slight tendency to warp. A sawmill and camp was established at about 5 miles east of Hawksbill Creek and the settlement that was built became known as Pine Ridge. Shortly afterwards $1\frac{1}{2}$ miles of 36in-wide narrow-gauge railway was constructed from the dock on the north coast to the settlement. Because of the exigencies of wartime most of the machinery of the lumber company was powered by steam with the hauling of the cut trees accomplished by steam skidding units (a kind of winch which could pull the felled trees to the railhead from as far as 1,000ft away). The cutting of the lumber was by steam-powered circular saws and the movement of the sawn lumber was by steam locomotive. For personal transportation a pumpcar was used with four men working hand pumps to propel the vehicle. The company owned about fifteen miles of railway track, most of which was in continual process of being laid down and taken up as the frontier of the lumbering operation proceeded eastwards. One of the first spans of the railway was laid from Pine Ridge to near Smith's Point on the south coast.

The method of lumbering was highly organised. A path was first blazed for the saw-team. The two-man team then cut all the trees in this area of over 8in girth at waist height. If any trees were felled outside the allotted area the tally man would not count them. The saw-men would then lop the branches off the felled tree and move on. After the saw-men a team of about eight men on the skidding units would fasten a cable and pull three or more trees to the railway track where they were stored in piles and from where they were loaded onto a flat car and taken to the sawmill. In its heyday Pine Ridge boasted two permanent sawmills, mills Nos 3 to 7 were mobile and No 8 was another permanent mill erected in the area today known as Buckingham

80

County. At the sawmills the lumber was converted into weatherboarding, planks and rectangular section beams up to 12in square and 30in long. Most of the wood was exported of course, though it was locally used in the construction of West Side village in Freeport and the Grand Bahama Hotel in West End.

Before the war Wallace Groves, a Virginian financier, came to settle in the Bahamas. He bought Little Whale Cay in the Berry Islands and created an island paradise out of this limestone atoll. He learned much about how an island community is brought into being which was knowledge he put to good use later on in life. In 1946, after studying the colony for investment opportunities, he gambled his capital and bought the ailing Abaco Lumber Company. With the lumbering rights to Grand Bahama, as well as Abaco, Groves set about modernising the operation. In a short while he replaced all the steam equipment (except the locomotives) with diesel-driven machinery and, aided by much of the original staff, he soon put the company on its feet.

A year after the ownership of Abaco Lumber changed hands, the island experienced the worst hurricane in living memory which created an excessively high tide and which marooned the west end of the island. Mercifully no one was killed. In the aftermath of the storm the islanders started picking up the pieces. Standard Oil, who had shortly before been granted a concession to prospect for oil on Grand Bahama, started by rebuilding the dock at West End. This company explored the island very thoroughly for three years for evidence of oil in the substrata, but as far as anyone knows their findings were negative. As a souvenir of their brief presence at Grand Bahama a few rotting metal structures can be seen on the Little Bahama Bank at low tide.

In February 1949 we have a first-hand account of Grand Bahama from Evans Cottman, the author of *Out Island Doctor*. On a periodic visit to the island he recalls anchoring midway down Hawksbill Creek in his boat the *Green Cross* and being greeted by an armada of dinghies from the settlements of Pinder's Point and Eight Mile Rock. He established his clinic in a small vaulted structure on the ocean front near the present bunkering line, which building had previously served as a missionary hospital for Dr Stratton, another medical man licensed by the Government to serve as an 'Unqualified Medical Practitioner' in the out-islands. The two communities he had come to visit were quite tiny at this time, being overshadowed by the Grand Bahamian mushroom city of Pine Ridge. Whilst on the island Dr Cottman was offered the temporary post of camp doctor by the Abaco Lumber Company. With a plane from Marsh Harbour to Pine Ridge every week Dr Cottman felt he would be able to keep in touch with his adopted home in Abaco, so he accepted. His temporary job turned out to be hectic however, and he treated patients with an endless series of breaks, bruises and burns and, as his clientele put it colourfully, plagued with 'gas and wombs troubles'—a term that covered everything from tumours to gonorrhoea! One day after he had completed some kitchen surgery, he was startled by a small terror-stricken boy who cried at him, 'Come quick to de clinic, Doctuh! De locomotive run over de brakeman! He on de porch and his liver's in his hat!' The statement was only a slight inexactitude in fact, since the engine had rolled over the torso of the unfortunate man so that his pulverised lungs had filled his toppled hat to the brim. How often Dr Cottman got to Marsh Harbour during these hectic months he does not say. However, help came at last in the form of Dr Ejnar Gottlieb, a German doctor who was to be the permanent medical practitioner of Pine Ridge. He inherited the small clinic and the never-ending task of tending to the sick and patching and mending broken skin and bones, especially after the rum had been flowing.

With the improved output due to mechanisation Abaco Lumber expanded its operation and in 1951 was awarded a contract from the National Coal Board in Britain to provide them with pit props. It was at this time Mr Groves re-negotiated his concession with the Government to permit the lumbering of 6in and later 4in girth trees. The Grand Bahama pine was admirably suited for pit props since the minor warping of the wood would not be a serious detriment in a coal mine tunnel and it had excellent compressive strength. The pit props were supplied in varying girths of $4\frac{1}{2}$, $6\frac{1}{2}$ and 9in diameter. About thirty-five cargoes of pit props averaging 1,500 fathoms and 200 standards of lumber were shipped to England and two shiploads arrived in Germany from the south shore slip (now the harbour). Prior to this time it had been necessary to load the timber on barges on the north side of the island and tow them out 30–40 miles to where ships could wait in deeper water along the edge of the Little Bahama Bank. To facilitate the movement of the lumber a permanent railway link was installed between Pine Ridge and the slip in 1952.

About this time Dr Cottman was back at Pine Ridge, filling in for Dr Gottlieb who was taking a well-deserved holiday with his wife in Germany. With the new contract from the National Coal Board several hundred workmen from Andros, Cat Island and the Turks Islands were brought in to work on the lumbering operation. Though they were housed in separate areas at Pine Ridge, there was much friction between the islanders which reached a crescendo of bedlam after paytime on Saturday. As ever, love and alcohol aggravated the situation and Dr Cottman, doubtless with some exaggeration, recalls that at times it seemed as if there was a race to see if he could patch up a cut as fast as they could make one.

The lumbering operation was seldom without incident. The company could boast one of the only railways in the Bahamas (there was another in Inagua) and two magnificent, antediluvian, single-cylinder steam upright locomotives. One eventful day in 1948, however, locomotive No 5 became no more. It seems that Dick the driver shut off the safety valve to build up the boiler pressure to negotiate an incline on the return trip to Pine Ridge. Towards the end of his mid-day meal the driver remembered the closed valve and rushed to the engine. The driver did not know that the boiler was dry when he took on more water. In seconds it was all over. Locomotive No 5 'blowed up', as one eye witness put it, with the sound of a thunderclap. Dick the driver was never seen again and four other people were killed in the explosion. The official inquiry that ensued placed the blame on human error.

In its heyday the Abaco Lumber Company on Grand Bahama was the largest single employer in the Bahamas with about 1,800 people on the payroll, and in fact in 1953 the community of Pine Ridge comprised 1,668 inhabitants, or more than three times the population of the next largest settlement at West End.

BIRTH OF TOURISM

In the post-war period the Bahamas made great strides to establish tourism in the colony and Nassau soon became a universally known vacation paradise. The out-islands, with no hotels or resort facilities, remained largely unvisited except by occasional yachts. Sensing the potential of the out-islands, Billy (later Sir Billy) Butlin explored the Bahamas with a view to constructing a holiday village to tap the American vacation market. The site he chose was almost the nearest point of the Bahamas to the Florida mainland : West End, Grand Bahama.

Butlin bought up a large tract of land at the tip of the island in 1948 and proceeded to build 'Butlin's Vacation Village', with a view to providing complete vacations for middle-income families at a very moderate room rate. He formed a public company incorporated in the Bahamas and was supported by several large British companies. Shares to the extent of some £2 million ($10 million at that time) were issued. The Reema Construction Company from England acted as general contractors for the work and ground was broken in 1949. Work went ahead and more and more construction staff moved in, necessitating the building of temporary accommodation, called the 'European Quarters', some half a mile from the main project. (Some of these buildings are still standing, illustrating the truism that there are few things more permanent than a temporary building.) But due to the dock strike in Britain, which lasted for over three months, materials and supplies were held up, seriously impeding the progress of the work. In addition to the expatriate staff, a large number of Bahamians

84

were employed on the construction work and a labour camp was built which housed some 800 people. Anticipating the idea would appeal to thousands of Americans, Butlin planned to build several large chalets, an airstrip, power plant, conference halls, a dock, swimming pools and shops. In fact the project was to become a self-contained 'holiday camp' after the English model. As there were no scheduled airlines and the airstrip was not completed, most of the staff and workers came in by boat or by chartered sea-plane. Transportation to and from the island was a major problem, though given time to promote the hotel further the transportation facilities could easily have been provided.

Eventually after some long delays and setbacks the holiday village was opened on 15 February 1950, even though the construction work was not complete. The plans called for 500 rooms accommodating 1,000 people, but only half that amount could be accommodated when the doors finally opened. The cost of a week's vacation was a moderate $99 and for some of the time the hotel was full. In July 1960 Butlin told the *Miami News* that he expected to have the entire holiday village finished in time for the winter season. However, mainly due to the cost of construction, the project was not paying its way and it had a number of jittery creditors. In autumn 1950 some of them came over to West End and 'posted' the area and had it closed down. The holiday village had only been open some ten months. The bulk of the staff were repatriated and only five caretakers and a small labour force of fifty men were all that was left operating. Eventually the whole project was put under the hammer by the Supreme Court and was sold to one of the largest creditors in England. The creditors formed Grand Bahama Properties Ltd to administer the assets which were shortly thereafter taken under option by a group out of Chicago. A final date was agreed upon for this group to take up their option but it did not materialise, for at about the same time a front page article appeared in the *New York Herald Tribune* stating that the group was supposedly connected with 'Murder Incorporated'—a sinister US gang of professional murderers. It was also rumoured that they intended to introduce a gambling operation on Grand Bahama. The reputation of the group was soon common knowledge and reaction was immediate —no more was ever heard of the Chicago syndicate.

The original company of Butlins (Bahamas) Ltd had an option to purchase some 20,000 acres of Crown Land as an incentive for them to develop the holiday village. In order to keep the option open the hotel was re-opened around 1955 after extensive alterations and repairs had been made and Grand Bahama Properties ran the hotel as a high-class fishing resort. But, being primarily interested in the real estate business, they let it be known that the hotel was for sale. There was speculation, particularly in London, that the Bay Street oligarchy of Nassau was less than helpful in the matter of supporting Butlin's venture. There was a chance in 1955 that if a full gambling licence had been issued to a reputable organisation it might have helped put the hotel on its feet, but it was thoroughly quashed by the press in Nassau. Certainly the transportation to and from the hotel was a major unsolved problem, then the dock strike in England and the devaluation of sterling at this time were serious setbacks. Another often repeated reason for the failure of the project was that the holiday camp idea was unpopular with Americans though there seems to be little evidence of this. Certainly the 'americanisation' of the venture would have been a simple enough task. On the evidence at hand one may conclude that it was essentially the right development in the right place—but it was about ten years too soon.

While Butlin was struggling at West End the Americans were moving into Gold Rock Creek to create a Missile-Tracking Station under the Destroyer-Bases Accord of 1940, and in so doing they made Grand Bahama part of what was called the 'billion dollar shooting range'. Consolidated Construction of Nassau were the contractors for the project, which consisted of an airstrip, living quarters and several radio electronic and radar installations for the United States Air Force who ran the station.

After the demise of the Butlin venture the island fell back again on hard times. The experience of Douglas Silvera (later a director of the Grand Bahama Port Authority) is indicative of the primitive state of the island at the time. On his first visit as an employee of Consolidated Construction his survey party landed in a seaplane on the north coast since there was no airstrip on the island. From there the party journeyed by pump car to Pine Ridge and thence onwards they travelled by the incredibly bumpy road to Gold Rock (Helweg Larsen, the author of *Columbus Never Came*, hardly exaggerated when he said the road 'had more dangerous potholes than there are stars in the heavens'). From Gold Rock they were to continue on to High Rock by boat where the survey party were to camp. The sea to the south of the island was true to its reputation, and when only a few hundred yards from the shore, the two skiffs in which they were sailing both caught a fluky gust of wind and capsized simultaneously. Survey instruments, tents and personal effects were washed overboard which they retrieved by skin diving in the sea. They then swam to shore and radioed another seaplane from the base and travelled the remaining 7 miles to High Rock in a plane chartered from Nassau 140 miles away! Dr Cottman recalls he was lucky to avoid a sequel to the experience of Douglas Silvera about this time when he took a trip with ol' John of High Rock to Sweeting's Cay. Ol' John, who was in a very tipsy state, unleashed 35yd of canvas on a dinghy on a similarly blustery day, and for 20-odd miles he dodged rocks and swigged rum (until he dropped the bottle accidentally overboard), finally transporting the terrified medical man to the solace of Sweeting's Cay.

Meanwhile, perhaps prompted both by his own involvement on the island and that of Butlin at West End, Wallace Groves started thinking about diversifying his investment on Grand Bahama. The lumber operation was a 'going concern' and he had made Little Whale Cay into a veritable paradise complete with a manor house, village, harbour, church and school. His idea fermented for several years until a rather remarkable man, the Earl of Ranfurly, was appointed governor in 1958. Lord Ranfurly is well known in the Bahamas for his involvement in civic projects which culminated in the Ranfurly Homes for

Children and the Out-Islands Mobile Library Service, but he also acted as mentor to Wallace Groves. After Groves sold the lumber operation and part of the timber concession he went to the Government with a plan which, if it succeeded, would go down in Bahamian history. When all Nassau thought Groves had to be slightly mad, Lord Ranfurly offered the moral support to give him faith to risk all and take the plunge. The 'plunge' was the incredible task of creating a new city on Grand Bahama Island.

Page 89 Bahamian personalities: *(top left)* Joseph Bevin, one-armed octogenarian of Rocky Creek; *(top right)* Mrs Joseph Bevin characteristically smoking; *(below left)* Drusila Laing of Pelican Point with small green turtle; *(below right)* Junkanoo drummer

Page 90 Early inhabitant: Arawak Indian girl. The Lucayan Indians were closely related to the Arawaks

6 THE HAWKSBILL CREEK
AGREEMENT

IN the early 1950s tourism had started to become very popular in the Bahamas but the idea of selling property (except
to a handful of upper-income people) had hardly been ex-
ploited and the encouragement of industry to the colony was all
but wishful thinking. Nevertheless with rare foresight this was the
time that Wallace Groves decided to sell the lumber rights to part
of Grand Bahama in order to concern himself with a greater
plan. But first a buyer had to be found. After some time a nibble
became a bite and Mr Groves was offered a million dollars more
than he privately valued the lumber rights. A handshake agreement was made but the intending buyer died suddenly of a heart
attack on his way to finalise the deal. It can be imagined therefore
with what relief another offer was considered a few weeks later.
This time the interested party was the giant National Container
Corporation of the United States and shortly thereafter the deal
was quickly consummated for a reported $4 million.

Sir Stafford Lofthouse Sands, then Minister of Tourism in the
Bahamas, acted as Mr Groves's lawyer throughout this transaction
and so it was natural that he should look to Sir Stafford for the
legal expertise needed to conceive his bold plan : the development of a 'free port' community in the pine barren island of
Grand Bahama. Fourteen years later, Mr Groves was so successful in his venture that he was characterised by Robert Wilder in
his best-selling novel *An Affair of Honour*, as Max Hertog who
boasted that he was 'going to buy up Grand Bahama . . . and
build a town and call it Freeport'. But Wilder, in painting a
picture of the creator of Freeport as a blustering tycoon, was far

F

from reality since Wallace Groves was in character an exceptionally reserved man who, without fanfare, took a calculated but nevertheless enormous business risk, with very limited capital considering the project he had in mind. What perhaps is most remarkable, is that he was prepared to gamble his fortune on a project which had such high risk and complexity.

EARLY 'FREE PORTS'

The 'free port' idea was not new in the Caribbean. A 'free port' generally permits the importation and sale of goods without the onus of customs or excise duty. Regulations differ from place to place and it was not unusual to favour one nation over another. Sometimes specific items were excluded from the 'free port' privileges and the sale of goods to local residents was often prohibited. In the eighteenth century England had made a plan for the establishment of 'free ports' in the western hemisphere which, it was hoped, 'would drain away the bullion of New Spain from Cadiz to Great Britain'. Dominica and Jamaica were the first 'free ports' established by Britain though the Bahamas were discussed as being a suitable location.

During the second term of Woodes Rogers, a man named John Ker had the original idea of establishing a 'free port' on New Providence. Ker, however, was cheated out of his idea by the speaker of the House of Assembly. The governor also found the speaker troublesome and, after having him arrested, the speaker was found guilty of sedition and find a crippling £750 and ordered to be detained during the king's pleasure until he could post a sufficient bond for his future good behaviour. However, the privately sponsored 'free port' idea fell into abeyance. Later a paper sent from the Privy Council and signed by Pitt included a suggestion for the creation of 'free ports' on the Dutch pattern in the Bahamas and Bermuda. In George III's reign Nassau was for a time a partial 'free port' and permitted some of the produce of foreign colonies to be admitted in the Bahamas in foreign vessels 'under the usual regulations for "free ports" ', but even before the Napoleonic War, the idea was abandoned in the Bahamas and remained so for over a century and a half.

THE HAWKSBILL CREEK AGREEMENT

On 4 August 1955 the Hawksbill Creek Agreement was signed by the Hon A. G. H. Gardner-Brown, Acting Governor of the Bahamas, and Mr Wallace Groves, President of the Grand Bahama Port Authority Ltd. The Agreement allowed the Port Authority (a private company, the majority of whose shares were owned by Abaco Lumber Company in the person of Mrs Groves) certain rights and privileges within the area designated as the 'Port Area'. For its part the Port Authority covenanted to create a harbour and develop an industrial community on Grand Bahama. The Government guaranteed to the Port Authority and its licensees that non-consumable items could be imported into the Port Area free of customs duty and it further agreed that there would be no excise, export or stamp taxes for the continuance of the Agreement; that is to say for ninety-nine years. It also guaranteed that for thirty years after the signing of the Agreement (later extended by five years to 1990) there would be no real estate taxes, personal property taxes or taxes levied against the Port Authority or its licensees on earnings in the colony. It further went on to vest the Port Authority with the right to administer the Port Area, exclude undesirables, to plan the Port Area and to license persons or businesses. Some of these heads of Agreement have been changed or subsequently amended, a matter which is taken up later.

The Hawksbill Creek Agreement is a contractual document between the Port Authority and the Bahamas Legislature acting on behalf of the British Crown. It bears a likeness to such historic agreements as those made by the Crown with Hudson's Bay Company which was responsible in large measure for the early development of British Canada. Simply stated, the Hawksbill Creek Agreement is a rather straightforward declaration of concessions granted by the Bahamas Government in return for certain commitments from the developers. Financially it is difficult to see how the Government could have been out of pocket on account of the Agreement since all expenses incurred by Government were to be reimbursed, and even the conveyance of the original 50,000 acres of land was subject to a conditional purchase lease which could be revoked in case of non-performance. The administration of the Port Area could be said to have been 'government by contract'. To encourage industry the guarantees concerning import duty, income, corporation and real estate taxes, were later enhanced by the construction of a commodious harbour, the provision of power, water and telephone services and the psychic advantage of being located in the millionaires' playground of the Bahama Islands. An important feature of the Agreement was the implicit power vested in the Port Authority to license other businesses which, as originally intended, allowed them to operate almost without any reference to the Government. The Royal Commission Report on Freeport published in 1971 noted that the power to grant licences is nowhere expressly conferred by or under the Agreement though, it suggests, it undoubtedly recognised its existence. And as for the licence fees the Report infers that the 'licensees thought them an acceptable levy for the privilege of carrying on their undertaking in Freeport and for the protection against undue or inordinate competition which was afforded them by the Port Authority through its licensing policies'. A person or business thus licensed took on many of the same responsibilities and obligations as the Port Authority. Legal opinion held that the Government of the Bahamas, as it was then constituted, could not repeal or alter the Agreement unilaterally without consent of the British Crown.

The original Hawksbill Creek Agreement envisaged the encouragement of industries to Grand Bahama Island and the early development reflected this intention. The harbour was the first focus of attention and it was here that the fortuitous unfolding of events permitted the undercapitalised Port Authority to create the deepwater harbour called for in the Agreement. Mr D. K. Ludwig, the shipping magnate, was at that time re-negotiating a ship-building contract in Japan and was having difficulty in agreeing upon the terms and so he conceived the fantastic idea of creating a major shipbuilding yard in Grand Bahama using, presumably, Japanese labour. Under an agreement with the Port Authority he dredged the harbour in exchange for 2,000 acres of industrial land. By thus having shown that he was serious, the Japanese relented on some of their conditions and Mr Ludwig continued to have his ships built in Japan, which some assume was his intention all along. His company, National Bulk Carriers, cur-rently own and have on order some of the largest supertankers in the world. As the *Bahamas Handbook* pointed out, for a time it was thought that Freeport had got a $2 million harbour out of Ludwig for nothing. But then the news broke that the shipping tycoon had sold his harbour-side land at Freeport to a subsidiary of the United States Steel Company at a price which at least recaptured his original investment. The reason for shelving the shipyard plans was explained somewhat implausibly by Bahamas Shipyards' general manager at the time : 'we discovered that the mechanical plans we had drawn up just didn't suit the island's geological structure'. Mr Ludwig continued his interest in the island, however, and came back later as a major real estate developer.

Despite having fulfilled the obligation to dredge the harbour, the early industrial development of Freeport was very slow. The early tasks of the Port Authority concerned the purchase of land from private owners and the provision of roads and utilities for the early population of Freeport—estimated to be a paltry 150 persons in 1956. The only international airport on the island was at West End which was reached by way of a graded road con-structed and maintained by the United States Government (in connection with a series of missile-tracking sites from Hope Town Bight to Pelican Point which the United States leased on the island under the Destroyer-Bases Accord). Hawksbill Creek had to be crossed by a wooden bridge which replaced a 'logwalk' of the earlier part of the century, and eastwards from there the only driveable road was the old logging trail which was deeded to the Government and became Queen's Highway and later the Grand Bahama Highway of today. The principal settlement in the 'Port Area' was Pine Ridge which had a population of about 1,500 people where the Government maintained a post office and customs and immigration office (which building was later barged to Abaco) and a wireless telegraph station.

It was at this time the Governor, the Earl of Ranfurly, KCMG, the then Governor of Jamaica, Sir Hugh Foot (later Lord Caradon —British Ambassador to the United Nations) and Mr Wenzel Granger, MBE (later Chief Immigration Officer of the Bahamas), visited Mr Groves to hear first-hand of his latest plans for Grand Bahama. Lord Ranfurly must have been impressed because he was quoted on this occasion as saying that the Freeport project had more merit and greater potential than any other scheme ever to be proposed in the Colony—but this prediction fell on deaf ears.

By 1955 the island had been lumbered as far as Gold Rock Creek when Mr Groves entered into the agreement with the National Container Corporation to sell the lumber rights to the remainder of the island. The National Container Corporation, which later became a subsidiary of the giant Owens (Illinois) Company moved the base of their operations to North Riding Point and many of the buildings from Pine Ridge were transported by trailer to this isolated headland on the north coast where relatively deep water approached the shore. To serve as an office, commissary and doctor's consulting rooms an odd vessel from another age was acquired and docked at North Riding Point. The paddle steamer the PS *Robert Fulton*, just a short while before on the Hudson river, New York, had found a new lease of life by making a bizarre appearance at the south of Little Bahama Bank.

The National Container Corporation, as their name suggests, were involved in making cardboard boxes among other things, and so the Grand Bahama pine took the ultimate relegation of a lumber tree. Having once been made into structural timber, then into pit props, it now ignominiously became a pulp. Pine Ridge was gradually 'phased out' though Groves and 'Natcon' had made an agreement to create a deep-water slip at the southern end of Hawksbill Creek to serve the lumber operation. This slip was subsequently sold back to Mr Groves at an undisclosed amount. After a year on the north coast the National Container Corporation moved once again, this time away from Grand Bahama completely, to Snake Cay, Abaco.

With the winding down of Pine Ridge the focus on the community moved to the harbour where Groves was already established in a small concrete block and stucco building called, on account of its flamingo hue, the 'pink house'. Next door, so to speak, Jan Porel, an early confidant and adviser of Groves, lived in a green house of similar unpretentious design. A few wooden houses, a barracks, and a commissary were built in the harbour area and were incidentally amongst the last buildings on the island to be constructed of native lumber. A temporary police station was established and a branch of Barclays Bank opened its doors to customers. Later the same year, three miles away, in the middle of the pine barren, work started on 'down-town' Freeport.

In the two years that followed, a certain amount of consolidation took place; small businesses were licensed, roads were constructed, an airstrip was started, small offices and shops were built and housing areas were developed. However, progress was undeniably slow. Sensing the situation an interview was arranged between Charles Hayward, a wealthy British industrialist and chairman of Firth Cleveland group of companies, and Mr Groves. The meeting was timely for Mr Hayward bought a 25 per cent interest in the Port Authority for £1 million which he called at the time 'a tangible expression of faith in the undertaking'. Groves then arranged the sale of another 25 per cent of the stock of the company to a New York consortium headed by investment banker Charles Allen. The fresh capital was much needed and helped to buy time until the venture could be said to be 'over the top'.

SHIP BUNKERING

In 1958 a major project was commenced when the Port Authority started to build a ship-bunkering oil depot near the harbour. The Freeport Bunkering Company was formed and Gulf Oil Company lent $1 million for the construction of the terminal. In the first eighteen months of operation business was much slower than expectations, but in March 1960 Freeport received a windfall. The US Government, bowing to Texas oil interests, imposed a quota on all residual fuels that could be imported into the United States. The major oil companies discovered that it paid them to bunker their ships in Freeport in order to carry other fuels to the USA to the extent permitted by law. The result was dramatic. In one month in December 1961 the terminal exported 922,000 barrels of duty-free oil mainly to United States coastal shipping but also to an increased number of ships on the Caribbean–United States. The major oil companies discovered that it paid them ships would be waiting for their turn to take on fuel at the two off-shore moorings, from the two oil barges or alongside the wharf. The fuel supply to the terminal was effected by tankers bringing bunker fuels from Venezuela. Grand Bahama's strategic position at the intersection of the Northwest Providence Channel and the Gulf Stream was partly the key to the bunkering operation's success since it allowed both coastal vessels and trans-Atlantic ships en route to and from the Panama Canal to avail themselves of the terminal where water, provisions, as well as fuel oil, could be taken on board.

EARLY DEVELOPERS OF FREEPORT

The main contractor on the harbour and bunkering terminal was a Freeport licensee, Marine Construction and Engineering Company Ltd, which firm was associated with Diamond Construction of Savannah, Georgia. Among the other companies in operation before 1960 were Freeport Construction Company Ltd, a building and heavy construction company 50 per cent owned by the Port

Authority and about thirty other licensees engaged in subcontracting and service industries. A few licensees were over ambitious and were early failures. Bahamas Seacraft Ld, one of the first licensees, built a vast warehouse on Hawksbill Creek for the manufacture of motor cruisers though they subsequently abandoned the venture. Another failure was a farm operation which cleared and cultivated 1,000 acres of land near Pine Ridge for cucumbers and tomatoes. The financial success of the farming venture depended on an untimely frost in Florida thus creating a demand for imported produce at premium price. After two seasons of waiting for the illusive frost the owners of the farm ploughed in a complete crop only two weeks before a frost did in fact hit Florida which, had they lasted out, would have made their gamble worthwhile. It is interesting to note that the manual workers were almost entirely Haitians brought in with Government approval for the job under the labour clause of the Hawksbill Creek Agreement.

About 40 miles of road had been cut by this time and the newly completed harbour admitted the first ship on 7 November 1959 —the Greek 7,268 ton, 441ft long SS *Samos*. Building development too was proceeding apace. The Port Authority commissioned Alfred Browing Parker, the well-known Florida architect, to design an airport terminal, a school (later to become St Paul's School), and an administration office building and an eight-cottage guest unit known as the Caravel Club. Parker also designed distinguished private houses for Mr Diamond, Mr Groves and Mr Jack Hayward, the son of Charles Hayward who later gained much publicity for his donation of Lundy Island to the National Trust and for financing the towing of SS *Great Britain* from the Falkland Islands to England. The vast Groves and Hayward houses were a bonanza for the embryo building industry of Freeport since up to that time the community had the appearance of a small construction camp in the pine barren. These houses, after Government House in Nassau, were two of the largest residences to be constructed in the Bahamas. However, apart from the Caravel Club and the Fishing Hole guest house and restaurant the island had no vacation facilities for visitors. The *Bahamas Handbook* quoted Mr Groves as saying 'many visitors have expressed interest in vacationing here, but we just haven't room for them'. The years that followed were to change all that.

EARLY SOCIAL LIFE IN FREEPORT

Small as the community was in those days, like so many pioneer settlements, there was a great community spirit among the early residents. With only temporary electric power, erratic telephone service and no shops, the residents looked to each other for entertainment. In 1960 only 305 (or 7 per cent) of the Grand Bahama population was white, 3,340 were black and the remainder of mixed race or Asiatics. In a report written this same year, Cornell University noted that there was complete integration of the few public facilities of the island though they noted 'there was virtually no intermixture of racial groups at the personal or social level'.

One of the first community institutions for the white population was the Freeport Garden Club which acted as a most important diversion for the Freeport housewives in the early pioneering days. The club made valiant efforts to turn the pine barren into a Garden of Eden, and though they were unequal to the task, a few areas of Freeport bear evidence of their perseverance. In 1961, at the instance of Jack Hayward, another club was formed: the Freeport Players Guild. This club was to make perhaps the most important cultural contribution to Freeport to date. The first play performed was *The Paragon* which played before a capacity audience of thirty people for two nights in the only available classroom of the Freeport School. However, despite the attempts to make a new community livable, the lack of diversions was a serious drawback and the pristine rawness of Freeport in the early days was even too much for some industrialists, the six 'No's' of the Hawksbill Creek Agreement notwithstanding, i.e. no income taxes, no capital gains taxes, no real estate taxes, no personal property taxes, no excise taxes, no customs duties (except on goods for personal consumption). An internationally famous rum company thought very seriously of locating a plant in Freeport but the dearth of hotels, restaurants and other community facilities persuaded them to choose Nassau.

Elsewhere on the island things were also slowly starting to move. In West End after the abortive beginning of the Butlin's Vacation Village and subsequent attempts to make it a going concern, word was out in 1959 that the hotel was being sought by some American hoteliers. There were two prospective customers. Holiday Inns of America had sent in an architect to study plans for the renovation of the hotel but they preferred only to lease the property; however, another group wanted to purchase and shortly afterwards negotiations between Charles A. Sammons, a Dallas financier and principal stockholder of the Jack Tar Hotel chain, resulted in the acquisition of the property. The facilities were further renovated and extended. In a matter of months from the time of take-over, literally tons of building materials, furnishings and equipment were ferried from the mainland by means of landing craft, freighters and planes. The Jack Tar Company, cognisant of the transportation problem which had bedevilled Butlin, also acquired a small passenger liner, the MV *Grand Bahama*, to ferry passengers to and from the United States.

At the same time the 20,000 acres of land under option to Grand Bahama Properties was re-surveyed and it was revealed that only half of the land between West End and Holmes Rock was in fact usable. This area was then split up into tracts of some fifty acres subdivided and put on the market, followed by the small acreage tracts north of the Government Road. An interesting project which was to be a prototype of canal construction of the island was started at Bootle Bay, some three miles from West End. This development was created out of the low-lying swashland behind the sand dunes of the south coast where an entrance channel was dredged to create access to the sea and several feeder canals were dug. It was a development which showed great faith in the future of Grand Bahama after the debacle of the Holiday Camp some years previously. Linton Rigg, a yachtsman visitor, writing about this time predicted that Grand Bahama might 'even become the most important island in the Bahamas from the commercial point of view'. He also noted what an astute banker had to say about the Butlin holiday village : it will change hands several times but the third owner will make money—the prediction on both counts came true !

7   ISLAND ON THE MOVE

AS 1955 saw the birth of the Freeport venture so 1960 witnessed its coming of age. On 11 July of that year a further agreement, known as the Supplemental Agreement, was signed by the Government and the Port Authority. This Agreement acknowledged the accomplishments of the Port Authority and confirmed that the Port Authority had dredged the harbour channels, constructed a bunkering base and wharf, and complied with all the obligations of the Principal Agreement. It further granted to the Port Authority additional acreage of land at a nominal price north of the original 50,000 acres extending between Seagrape and Gold Rock Creek. In consideration of this it was mutually agreed that the original Hawksbill Creek Agreement would be amended by requiring the Port Authority to build a 200-room luxury hotel by 31 December 1963, to provide free education for school children living within the Port area, and it reaffirmed that the Port Authority was to continue to promote and encourage the establishment of lawful business enterprises in Freeport and (in clause 4) it makes an interesting reference to the possible establishment of future municipal government by way of a 'local authority'.

After the signing of the Supplemental Agreement lengthy three-cornered negotiations between D. K. Ludwig, US Steel Corporation and the Port Authority resulted in Freeport being chosen for the construction of a cement plant. Mr Ludwig was involved because part of his holding was implicated in the land transaction. The plant was to be owned by the Bahama Cement Company, a subsidiary of the giant US Steel Corporation, and in 1961 a site

103

was selected for the plant on the west side of the harbour. Limestone, the basic ingredient of cement, was to be obtained from the further dredging of the harbour and in course of time it was to make Freeport one of the largest artificially created harbours in the world. A concession was written into the Cement Company Agreement whereby the Bahamas Government guaranteed to the cement company a twelve-year monopoly on the manufacture of cement in the Bahamas.

At the same time as the cement plant agreement was being drawn up an even more important deal was being made. Louis Chesler, a dynamic Canadian financier who owned a controlling interest in Seven Arts, the motion picture studio, put together a number of financial interests which, together with the Port Authority, formed the Grand Bahama Development Company. Mr Groves, through the Port Authority, contributed 102,000 acres of land and Chesler with his associates put up $12 million in cash. This company claimed it would create a 'new riviera' in Freeport, and Vol 1, No 1, of the *Freeport News* of 6 October 1961 carried a story in which Wallace Groves declared that this was the largest land deal ever made in the Bahamas up to date. The Development Company land became known as 'Lucaya', and the Port Authority received one-half of the stock but did not control the company at the time.

Earlier in the year Grand Bahama Island had a brief moment of the international spotlight when Alan Bartlett Shepard, Jnr, was recovered from the sea and brought to the US Missile Base after making a suborbital flight of 302 miles from Cape Kennedy. The achievement did not match that of Yuri Gagarin of the Soviet Union, who in April 1961 had actually orbited the world but it was the first of several giant steps which put the United States into the race to landing a man on the moon. For most subsequent space shots including the historic flight of Apollo 11 Grand Bahama served as the first down-range station from Cape Kennedy.

It was after the formation of the Development Company that the building boom started in earnest in Freeport. In January 1962 the Freeport Trading Company, a large shipchandler, was established in the harbour to supplement the bunkering operation. Later construction started on the first canal development on the south shore, Bahama Terrace. Mr James Rand, inventor of the telephone dial system, philanthropist and the former president of Remington/Sperry Rand, came to live on the island on his yacht *Galaxy* which he berthed in Bahama Terrace. He had earlier founded the Colonial Research Institute in Freeport, the medical side of which became known as the Grand Bahama Clinic, though after his death in 1968 the name was changed to the Rand Memorial Clinic. Mr Rand donated a library to the community which he named, in honour of his *alma mater*, John Harvard Library.

To be built at the same time and adjacent to the new luxury hotel, work started on the Bell Channel Bay canal development which created more water-front building sites and a marina. During the excavation for the canals there was some excitement when the wreck of an old vessel (first thought to be a pirate ship, but more probably a lumber barge) was excavated from the swash-land. Bell Channel and subsequent canal construction have become the most dramatic man-made feature of the island. A temporary setback to the building boom occurred in July when the brand new airport terminal building was razed to the ground by fire. However, development elsewhere continued feverishly and shortly thereafter the first permanent church building was completed by the Anglicans and was dedicated by the Bishop of Nassau.

It came as no surprise when Harold DeGregory, the United Bahamian Party candidate for Grand Bahama and Bimini, was elected to the House of Assembly later that month. The United Bahamian Party (UBP) was elected to power by a very substantial margin and their return to power confirmed that in Freeport it would be 'business as usual'. Indeed the Port Authority was becoming knee deep in proposals, serious and bizarre, one of which went by the name of the 'Hong Kong West Project'. So serious was this proposal for a time that it gained recognition from the other side of the world when the *China Mail* of 20 October 1962 carried the headline :

ANOTHER 'HONG KONG' IS BORN
Colony's counterpart—complete with shops
restaurants and rickshaws—is
being constructed

The project was finally dropped, but sometime later the concept was resurrected and broadened to include several other countries —at which time the Chinese and the rickshaws failed to materialise due, no doubt, to problems concerning Chinese immigration to the island and the preference of people for motor vehicles!

The new year saw the introduction of a regular Mackay Airlines service with Florida. At the cement company plans were being finalised for the construction of a plan capable of producing up to one million tons of cement a year which was to include a Danish rotary kiln, giant silos and a specially equipped wharf for cement-carrying ships in the harbour area. The well-field area of the cement plant consisting of nearly 2,000 acres north of the main road to West End was dedicated as a wildlife sanctuary, and in April 1963 the Bahama Cement Company contract was let and work proceeded immediately on the $60 million facility.

But Freeport was not the only place to feel the impact of development on Grand Bahama. West End also enjoyed a minor 'boom'. In 1963 the Grand Bahama Hotel completed a large marina and network of canals. In August the Governor of the Bahamas, Sir Robert de Stapledon, opened the new airport terminal at West End by saying that in the old days for a man to make his mark in the Bahamas he must build a dock and in this day and age he must build a dock and an airfield—clearly in the governor's view the Jack Tar Hotel Company had made their mark.

In Freeport the luxury hotel called for in the Supplemental Agreement was finished on time and opened its doors to the world on New Year's Eve 1963. The Lucayan Beach Hotel, as it was

Page 107 Three denominations: *(right)* Anglican church, Freeport, first ecclesiastical building to be erected

(left above) Roman Catholic church of St Agnes at Seagrape; *(below)* the Hermitage, former Baptist church built at Barbary Beach, 1901

Page 108 Industry: *(above)* giant silos of the Bahama Cement plant on the west side of the harbour; *(below)* ships bunkering at new off-shore berth. Syntex plant, oil refinery and storage tanks in foreground

called, was indeed a luxury hotel with one facility no other hotel in the Bahamas could boast—inside it contained a large gambling casino. It was not the first casino to be permitted in the Bahamas under a Certificate of Exemption, but it was certainly the largest and best appointed. While the hotel was being built it was clear to Groves and Chesler that a lone hotel on a fairly undistinguished island would need some additional attraction and so the idea of a casino was conceived. Ministers of the ruling UBP were lobbied and the Certificate was granted by a narrow margin (the manner in which approval was obtained was to be the subject of a later Inquiry).

The rapid development of the Bahamas, and Grand Bahama in particular, soon caught the interest of the outside world. In February 1965 the *New York Times* published a derogatory report on the Bahamian political scene. And in the same month there was labour unrest at the hotels and one of the bunkering lines was sabotaged with the subsequent loss of hundreds of tons of bunkering oil into the sea. This event was shortly before a very popular opposition party politician named Lynden O. Pindling addressed a mass meeting in Freeport. His presence was timely, and he reminded his audience that though things were good they could be better, and he promised political reform as well as economic betterment. Two months later this same politician was to throw the speaker's mace out of the window of the House of Assembly in Nassau in defiance of parliamentary protocol and to bring attention to the unquestioned need for change. He was not to be disappointed.

In the midst of all the feverish activity, both economic and political, there came additional excitement. Four young divers discovered the remains of a sunken Spanish galleon loaded with treasure in under 10ft of water less than three miles from the Lucayan Beach Hotel, near a headland appropriately called Fortune Point. It is very possible that the wreck may have been the prize ship of Dutchman Piet Heyn which was shipwrecked in the seventeenth century without a trace. The divers first found an anchor which was unusual in that it did not have cross arms

G

which indicated that it came from a very early vessel. Later they located two cannons and silver coins in two, four and eight *reales* denominations. Experts subsequently identified the coins as Mexican in origin minted in a private house belonging to Hernando Cortés. The story was soon big news; a US paper carried a large headline reading '$9 MILLION DOLLAR TREASURE FOUND IN FREEPORT' and it went on to report that 10,000 silver coins—mainly in conglomerate form—had been found. The find was so large, in fact, that the numismatic asking price of the coins immediately went down, halving or quartering the estimated value (a later estimate placed the value of the coins at nearer $2 million). Then a series of unfortunate circumstances whittled the find down still further; besides the immediate devaluation, the Government quickly passed a law claiming 25 per cent of the spoils, but worse was to come. The youthful divers got so involved with the 'experts' and rival claimants who flocked to them, and also with bickering amongst themselves, that they ended up with almost nothing. The story is an object lesson in the pitfalls of easy money and has been recounted with candour and humour by one of the four divers, Jack Slack, in an appropriately named book called *Finders Losers*.

On 15 March 1965 Freeport held 'open house' to the members of Government and the Civil Service from Nassau. The occasion was the opening of the Bahamas Cement Company plant at which the Governor, Sir Ralph Grey, officiated with two other ex-governors in attendance: the Earl of Ranfurly and Sir Robert Neville. Speaking on behalf of Bahama Cement was Roger Blough, the Chairman of US Steel, who, a short time before, had gained a great deal of publicity by attempting to raise steel prices contrary to a directive by President Kennedy. In the afternoon Lord Ranfurly, the godfather of Freeport, presided over the opening of a traffic roundabout named in his honour, which was later to become the principal road intersection of the city—Ranfurly Circus.

In August of the same year the *Freeport News* included an interview with Mr Chesler concerning the transfer of the Development Company shares in which the Port Authority increased its holding to 54 (later 57) per cent and assumed full control of the Board. Mr Chesler indicated that 200,000 shares would change hands at $13.00 a share and an amount of shares 'considerably in excess of 300,000 would be placed in escrow' at a price close to $14 a share.

A year later 50,000 shares of Development Company stock was set for sale. It was reported that a substantial portion of the balance had been sold in a pre-offering with purchasers including London insurance companies and other investment institutions in Europe and South America. The names of the companies buying shares at the pre-offering were not revealed. Most of the shares sold belonged formerly to Louis Chesler. It was stated about this time that land sales for the year were expected in the region of $25–30 million or twice that of 1965.

AMENDMENT AGREEMENT

Meanwhile the Port Authority again went back to the Government for further amendment of the Hawksbill Creek Agreement which would become effective after four-fifths of the licensees had indicated their willingness to the proposed changes as provided for by the Agreement. After a preamble in which the Government acknowledged that the obligations of the Supplemental Agreement had been fulfilled, the Port Authority covenanted to build 1,000 low- and middle-income houses in Freeport (starting with 200 which were to be constructed within eighteen months of the signing of the Amendment Agreement). This provision encouraged lower-income workers for the first time to live in Freeport and it helped overcome the image of Freeport as an 'expatriate' community. Work started on a housing estate named 'Hawksbill' in April the following year. Additional provisions called for the Port Authority to build school accommodation for a total of 1,400 pupils and two clinics in Freeport and the surrounding settlements. Further the Port Authority was charged to extend the water lines to the settlements of Pinder's Point and Eight Mile Rock and pay £10,000 towards the cost of a town planning study for the Eight Mile Rock–Holme's Rock area. The Government in turn covenanted to operate the clinics and schools and for the future health and education of the community. By Christmas 80 per cent of the licensees had consented to the Amendment Agreement and on 1 March 1966 the Governor, Sir Ralph Grey (later Lord Grey, Governor-General of Northern Ireland), gave his seal of approval.

The Amendment Agreement is interesting because it takes account of the 'Greater Freeport' area which had been developing ever since the inception of Freeport. It is fairly clear from the statistics at hand that for every person migrating to Freeport at least one other person migrated into the villages outside Freeport. Nassauvians, Out-Islanders, Haitians and Jamaicans formed the bulk of the in-migration, though many non-Bahamians who arrived without proper papers were subsequently sent home.

WINDS OF CHANGE

In February 1966 Queen Elizabeth II paid an official visit to the Bahama Islands, which was the first time a ruling monarch had ever visited the colony. As part of the celebration three pavilions designed by architect Ray Nathaniels and called 'Bahamarama' were constructed in Nassau so that the out-islands could give the monarch a glimpse of life in the rest of the colony. A separate stand was allocated to Freeport/Lucaya and Mr Groves, Mr Hayward and other Port Authority officials were presented to the Queen and the Duke of Edinburgh. The imperial connection was continued when a month later the Royal Navy cruiser HMS *Tiger* paid a visit. The *Tiger* was the largest warship ever to have visited Freeport and shortly after she was to achieve public attention as the ship on which Prime Minister Wilson and Mr Ian Smith had a fruitless confrontation over the future of Rhodesia. And another vessel briefly associated with the island at this time was the 4,500 ton ship the *Wappen von Hamburg* (renamed the MV *Lucaya*) which was winding up an experimental three-month

112

daily ferry service between Freeport and Miami. This ship had previously been on the Hamburg–Heligoland run and had been leased by the Port Authority as an experiment to increase the number of tourists to the island. The experiment confirmed the need for such a vessel and the Port Authority shortly thereafter placed an order with a West German shipyard for an even larger ship capable of carrying roll on/roll off freight as well as passengers.

With an obviously important election in early January 1967, the *Wall Street Journal* sent down a couple of reporters to review the political scene in the colony; their three-part report was a bombshell. The *Wall Street Journal* of 5 October 1966 carried a front page article on the questionable politics of the ruling United Bahamian Party and made some very critical remarks about the Freeport venture, the status of the black majority and the nature of gambling in the Bahamas. The article earned the reporters a Pulitzer Prize. The highly respected *Economist* followed up with an article in their edition of 15 October headed 'Trouble in Paradise' with the theme 'Does the British Government Care?'. The effect of the articles almost certainly tipped the balance of the January election. On 10 January 1967 the Progressive Liberal Party (PLP) tied with the United Bahamian Party, having eighteen seats each in the House of Assembly. The sole Labour Party member threw his weight in with the PLP and the only other member, an Independent, became speaker of the House. For the bulk of the Bahamian populace it was as significant a year as 1834. The PLP with a slender and unreliable majority of one moved cautiously; education was to be fostered, a commission to study gambling was definitely to be instituted and the victorious black majority were to have more say, but otherwise they pledged 'not to rock the boat'. The mood at that time was well expressed by a Bahamian poetess, Susan Wallace :

> Stress on education,
> All gattie go to school,

'Cause dey can' 'ford de new Bahamian,
Ta be nobody fool.

An 'das de new Bahamian,
He head could hol' up high,
'Cause vict'ry make it possible,
Fa him to reach de sky.

Understandably the black majority were overjoyed yet incredulous at the PLP victory A few may have even been a little truculent at the outcome but it seemed that over a century after Emancipation their time had come at last.

8 CHANGE OF GOVERNMENT

THE Progressive Liberal Party headed by Lynden O. Pindling carried the Grand Bahama constituencies in the 1967 election. Warren Levarity, the member for western Grand Bahama and Bimini, was appointed to the cabinet with the prestigious post of minister of out-island affairs and Maurice Moore (aged 28 at the time), a relative newcomer to politics, became an important backbencher and representative for Freeport and eastern Grand Bahama. The first few months of the new Government were marked by bewilderment and apprehension on the part of foreign investors but assurances were given by Government spokesmen that no radical changes would be made. But as one frustrated commentator on the Bahamian political climate at the time complained: 'thoughtful assements of what is happening in the Bahamas are not easy to come by'.

The press continued to find the Bahamas good copy. On top of the bad publicity meted out by the two financial journals, the 'glossies' joined the hunt. The 1967 *The Saturday Evening Post* of 25 February carried a front cover photograph of a roulette table and the caption 'GAMBLING IN THE BAHAMAS : THE MAFIA AT WORK', and under the by-line of Bill Davidson eleven pages of largely unsubstantiated conjecture was reported in an article headed 'Shadow of Evil on an Island in the Sun'. Grand Bahama, he wrote, was a vast scar of raw white limestone as bulldozers cleared the way for another, more frenetic Miami Beach with hotel conference halls all ready to be converted into casinos. In point of fact at the time of writing no such conversions have taken place nor indeed are they likely.

115

GAMBLING COMMISSION

Later in the year the promised Commission on Gambling held court in Freeport and Nassau. The terms of reference of the Commission required them to take a close look at :

the suitability of persons employed in the casino;

the legislation and administration regarding casino gambling;

whether members of the Government had received pecuniary benefit from the introduction or operation of the casinos;

the accounting, calculating and distribution of profits of the casinos and the recipients thereof; and

any recipients of payments not disclosed in the accounts.

The Commission were able to air a lot of dirty washing in discovering irregularities, exposing undesirables and unravelling abstruse book-keeping. The Commission expressed considerable concern 'that the consultants who were members of the Council (the UBP Government) should ever have allowed themselves to be put in the position where a conflict of interest would surely have arisen'. The Commission suggested that gambling in the Bahamas be the subject of a Gaming Act supervised by a non-partisan Gambling Commission; that citizens of the United States should not be employed in any capacity directly involved with the gambling operation; and that the adult Bahamians be permitted to play at the casinos. By 1972 only the recommendation concerning the Gambling Commission has been put into effect.

The uncertainty of the future of Freeport was not improved by the sale of the telephone company and the only supermarket on the island to large American concerns and shortly after negotiations were begun for the sale of the Port Authority-owned taxi company and bunkering operation. The Port Authority was clearly steering a new course. Rumours were flying. In a front page article in the *Freeport News* of 27 January 1968, Mr Wallace Groves attempted to suppress the rumour that the Port Authority was about to be sold, but a month later the same paper announ-

ced : 'Groves swapping Port share for stock in Mining Company
—$80 million deal.' Despite the fact that it looked as if there had
in fact been a 'sell out' it was soon clear that the Port Authority
was a senior partner in the merger.

BENGUET CONSOLIDATED

This announcement referred to a preliminary agreement whereby
most of the shares of the Grand Bahama Port Authority would
be exchanged for Benguet Consolidated shares. Benguet was a
Manila-based public company, engaged principally in mining
gold and chrome-bearing iron ore in the Philippines whose shares
were listed on the New York Stock Exchange. The business community of Freeport were pleased with the idea that the Port
Authority was going 'public' since it brought international recognition to Freeport, allowed them to buy shares in their 'mother'
company and assured them that the Port Authority's actions
would be public and subject to standards demanded by the
United States Securities Exchange Commission. It seemed for a
time that the deal would not go through but in fact the Government used their bargaining power behind the scenes to stipulate
measures whereby the Port Authority would consult with
the Government before exercising its rights in the following
areas :

> exclusion of persons or vehicles from the Port Area,
> planning and laying out of the Port Area,
> before changing rates and charges for utility services; and
> before licensing new business enterprises.

A further provision was the standardisation of customs and
immigration procedures with the rest of the Bahamas. The
Government also bought 7·5 per cent equity in the company,
which amounted to 162,973 shares at $5.60 each, a total cost
of $912,649. In addition the Government requested the right to
audit the Port Authority's books and to appoint a director to
both the boards of the Port Authority and Benguet Consolidated.

117

For a brief while the Philippine Government held up ratification of the transaction on the grounds that another government was involved but it finally approved the merger in early 1969.

Working with only a slender majority the Progressive Liberal Party called for another election to receive a clearer mandate. The date set for the general election was 10 April 1968, and at that time the PLP were re-elected by the substantial margin of 29 seats to 5 UBP seats with Randol Fawkes as the sole representative of the Labour Party and Alvin Braynen, Independent, who became speaker of the House. The Hawksbill Creek Agreement had long been a source of contention but with a vastly increased majority behind them the Government was understandably determined to make Freeport a part of the new Bahamas, in economic and cultural terms as well as political. From that day forward the destiny of Freeport became inextricably part and parcel of the Bahama Islands as a whole.

Throughout the election period the hotels were full and licences continued to be issued. In fact, the day after the election there was a ground-breaking ceremony near Freetown for a motion picture studio and a month later Firth Cleveland started construction on a nineteen-storey apartment building which, for a time, was the tallest in the Bahamas. And shortly afterwards in Germany, Mrs Pindling, the wife of the re-elected Premier, launched the 14,000 ton MV *Freeport* which had been commissioned by the Port Authority and the US Freight Company to operate as a cruise ship and ferry between Miami and Freeport. It was in fact the climax of an era. In the first eighteen months of the new Government the development of the island, indeed the Bahamas, hit new heights, though it was clear that political changes were afoot.

During the election there had been much talk of independence and in September Premier Pindling led a multi-party delegation to London. The worst fears of the conservative UBP were not

118

realised, though the Government obtained several constitutional changes:

> a Bahamian minister would be appointed in charge of police though the ultimate responsibility for internal security would continue to rest with Britain;
> the Bahamian Government would be consulted before Britain appointed future governors;
> the Senate would be reconstituted and limited in its powers.

After this conference the colony became a 'Commonwealth' and the Premier took the title 'Prime Minister'.

Another matter that was discussed was that there would be a safeguard to investors of inconsistencies of future legislation— a very necessary clarification that the ground rules for carrying on business in the Bahamas were not to be changed, although the requested 'safeguard' did not find any indelible form in the Constitution. By the year's end it was clear that 'Bahamianisation' and 'Progress' (in that order) were the watchwords. At this time the *Newsletter* of Charles Darraugh appraised the investment and business outlook and predicted that most factors in the economy's high 1968 growth rate would carry over to the future with some fluctuations as the effects of the new policy became felt. All sectors of the economy of the Bahamas, he predicted, would show growth, with Freeport and Nassau being well out in front, and for a time this prediction seemed to be coming true. Understandably Darraugh was unable to anticipate the recession in the United States and the subsequent decline in investment that followed in 1970. Nevertheless by 1970 Freeport had a clear lead in the heavy industrial sector of the economy by possessing a cement-manufacturing plant, a bunkering terminal and the world's largest unit for the production of fuel oils of low sulphur content. The new industrial giant was named the Bahamas Oil Refining Company, the parent companies of which were the New England Petroleum Corporation (65 per cent) and Standard Oil of California (35 per cent), the latter being better known by its trade name: 'Chevron'. The $100 million refinery which incorporated the former bunkering facility was located just east of the harbour on a 600 acre site. In June 1970 the refinery started producing 250,000 barrels of fuel per day, intended mainly for use in the northeastern United States. The refinery announced that an extensive satellite petrochemical industry was expected to establish in Freeport, once the refinery was in full operation, which would use the naptha byproduct as the basic feedstock for petrochemical processing. The anticipated satellite industries include manufacturers of plastics, chemicals, fibres, detergents and synthetic rubber.

As if to confirm the industrial ascendancy of Freeport, the Bahamas produced a 6d (later 8 cent) postage stamp depicting the deepwater harbour with the caption 'Development'.

MOVE TOWARDS LOCAL GOVERNMENT

In 1968 a Harvard professor, Richard Musgrave, a tax consultant to the Government, suggested that the Bahamian real estate tax should be revised, made more equitable and enforced generally (Freeport excepted of course). His report went on to state that 'land is of unusual importance in the development of the Bahamian economy and a modest property tax on unused land will contribute to a more efficient pattern of land uses'. This report made it clear that the Government was looking for a fair and more universal system of taxation and for greater sources of revenue to support its ambitious social programme.

At about the same time a Government White Paper was released entitled 'Proposals relating to the Establishment of Local Government in the Out Islands of the Bahamas', which suggested the decentralisation of government from Nassau. This White Paper would allow local authorities (which could be composed of certain non-British subjects if popularly elected) to be responsible for the maintenance of all public ferries and roads (except trunk roads), general health and sanitation, town planning, liquor licensing, and so on. The revenue for these expenses would come out of the rates (real estate taxes) and such fees in whole or in part from licensing vehicles, bicycles, boats, shops, bars, etc.

West End and Eight Mile Rock on Grand Bahama should be early candidates for Local Authority status while Freeport, the White Paper points out, is 'eminently suited for the establishment of a Local Authority except for one factor' (the 'one factor' being the Hawksbill Creek Agreement). The White Paper continues, 'The Government will, of course, abide by the terms of this Agreement, but it was foreseen that the time would come when Freeport would have developed to the stage when some or all of its rights, powers and obligations under the Agreement should be transferred to a Local Authority.' But such a transfer could take place only with the agreement of the Port Authority, and the consent of 80 per cent of the licensees. The eastern half of the island, however, moved nearer to Local Government following a Government administrative review and a new eastern district was established at High Rock under a resident commissioner.

LICENSEE REVOLT

In March 1969 the effect of the Government's tightened grip on Freeport became felt when all re-entry (work) permits were called in and others were issued on payment of a fee. The newly formed Licensees Division of the Chamber of Commerce challenged the right of Government in this and the matter of the revised customs procedures and requested the Port Authority act to redress their grievances. The headlines in the *Grand Bahama Tribune* of 6 September 1969 read: 'Hundreds unanimous in decision to brief counsel—LICENSEES DECIDE TO FIGHT FOR RIGHTS BY ARBITRATION.' The licensees contended that the Port Authority had given the Government the rights to control immigration and licensing without reference to the licensees, many of whom had suffered disruption of business and loss of income. Another matter discussed as possible grounds for a law-suit was the matter of customs duty and tariffs. The newspapers reported that pledges of $100 and more were pouring into the Licensees' Division offices and a few days later, after a public meeting, Randol Fawkes, the former Minister of Labour, was retained as legal counsel.

In the height of this storm in a teacup the prime minister said of Freeport: 'In this city where, regrettably, almost anything goes, some economic opportunities have come to Bahamians. . . . [but they] . . . nevertheless are still the victims of an unbending social order which if it now refuses to bend must be broken.' In qualified support for Licensees' position Maurice Moore, parliamentary representative for Freeport, and C. A. Smith, the local chairman of the PLP, made their feelings public that all was not well in Freeport. After the PLP Conference in November that year, however, Mr Moore stated that 'government was making a genuine bid to solve the problem of Freeport' but Prime Minister Pindling, still rankled by the licensees' display of defiance, promised a 'determination' on the future of Freeport. The mood of the community was not improved by a series of raids by immigration officers and the police to round up illegal immigrants shortly after this time. Large numbers of people had been entering the Bahamas for years and illegally working without permits, so there can be no question that the authorities had a clear duty to remove all such illegal immigrants though the manner in which the raids were carried out became open to criticism in the press. Once a person has entered the Bahamas, inter-island traffic is unimpeded and Haitians, particularly, had been island-hopping their way to Grand Bahama ever since the founding of Freeport. As an example of this illicit traffic, in November 1969 an unseaworthy boat, the *Nassau Bottler* of 39·2 net tons, was intercepted landing Haitian nationals near Eight Mile Rock. Once ashore many of the passengers escaped into the bush, some were later recaptured by the police, but others were rapidly absorbed into the community. The small boat sank shortly after it completed its abortive mission.

In early February 1970 the Port Authority declared publicly that at the continued insistence of the licensees it would pay the legal fees for the arbitration proceedings. Clearly the Port Authority's position in this matter was that the Government imposed the new rules and so it was Government, not they, who was responsible for the situation. But within a matter of hours the Government made it clear that it was not going to tolerate such a challenge to its authority. A few days later the legislature announced that it was taking steps to amend the Hawksbill Creek Agreement where it considered it was contrary to the sovereign right of the Bahamas to control immigration. The 'determination' promised by the prime minister had come at last.

Throughout the period of the tripartite disagreement the financial climate of Freeport suffered. Some long-time residents of Freeport discovered that they could not obtain work permits, the largest plumbing company on the island went bankrupt, and in February 1970 the Freeport Savings and Loan Institution closed its doors in a behind-the-scenes effort to stave off insolvency. Even at West End the Grand Bahama Hotel closed down the marina as an economy move though it re-opened a few weeks later. The slump in business was followed by a certain amount of surliness on the part of the labour force and a wave of petty larceny broke out. The situation was further aggravated by the recession in the United States which slowed the flow of tourists visiting the islands. In an effort to assuage the decline which affected the entire country the prime minister launched a tourist courtesy campaign in March 1970.

During this period the new owners of Benguet Consolidated were rapidly reorganising their worldwide operations. In their 1969 *Annual Report* Benguet gave details of the source of its earnings: the income before extraordinary credit from the Bahamas operations was listed as $21 million and the income before the deduction of an unfavourable exchange variation in the Philippine operation was listed as $1·7 million. Adding the net income from these two sources to the retained earnings as of 1 January the retained earnings at 31 December were $77 million. In their *Annual Report* a year later Benguet Consolidated inserted a new note explaining the plan that Benguet intended to

123

adopt to conform to the Philippine law requiring that natural resource companies be 60 per cent Philippine owned. The report stated in part :

> To comply with Philippine law and separate the (Philippine and non-Philippine) operations, a plan was devised wherein a Panamanian corporation (Intercontinental Diversified Corp.) would be formed. Ultimately it would exchange all of its shares of the Port Authority and the shares of Benguet International, SA Benguet shareholders would exchange 85 per cent of their shares for all of their shares in Intercontinental. Then at least 60 per cent of the shares of Benguet would be offered for purchase to Philippine citizens. Management would proceed with the split-off of shares and separation of the operations subject to Philippine, United States of America and Bahamian regulatory agencies and approval of Benguet shareholders. After the completion of the split-off, Benguet would continue to own and operate the mines and other businesses located in the Philippines and Intercontinental would own and operate the Grand Bahama Port Authority Limited, Benguet International, SA and other businesses located outside the Philippines.

The shareholders agreed to this proposal in 1972.

Indicative perhaps of the changed times in July 1970, Mr Groves, in his seventieth year, the respected founder, principal executive and figurehead of the Port Authority, retired as chairman of the Board. His position was later taken by C. Gerald Goldsmith, a long-time business associate of Mr Groves. John T. Kimball, a relative newcomer from a large United States utility corporation, was appointed the new president of the Grand Bahama Port Authority and George Kates was appointed president of the Grand Bahama Development Company. Benguet had earlier in the year acquired about 20,000 acres of land in California and it became clear that there was a change in direction or, in the jargon of Wall Street, the company was 'diversifying its portfolio', though such diversification was clearly normal for a company with the size and potential of Benguet.

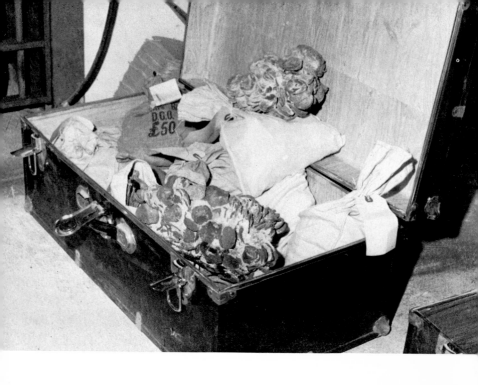

Page 125 Ancient and modern: *(above)* part of 'pieces of eight' treasure haul in bank vault; *(below)* Freeport Power Company plant with generating capacity of 60,125 megawatts

Page 126 Past and future: *(above)* one of the only two railways in the Bahamas. This locomotive, manufactured at York Iron Works, Pennsylvania, c. 1922, used to haul lumber. A single-cylinder steam upright engine, weighing six tons, exploded in 1948; *(below)* the telemetry installation near Gold Rock Creek, pointing, it could be said, ominously, to the sky

CHANGE OF GOVERNMENT

As a result of the events of 1969 and in an endeavour to have the full facts of the situation regarding Freeport properly investigated, the Bahamas Government announced that a Royal Commission would make a report on the future of Freeport. This news had a disturbing effect on the price of the stock of Benguet Consolidated. According to the *New York Times* the shareholders of Benguet flew into a 'tizzy' when the announcement was made and on 10 September the stock made the most active list with a 132,400 share turnover and finally closed a full point off for the day. It was reported that it would be the job of the Commission to review the development of the Freeport area since 1955 and make recommendations 'as to what changes, if any, ought to be made in terms of the Hawksbill Creek Agreement and subsequent amendments'. The report was submitted to the Government early in 1971 and was made public in the middle of that year.

The Report of the Royal Commission appointed on the Recommendation of the Bahamas Government to Review the Hawksbill Creek Agreement (to give the Report its full title) made several recommendations. The Commission concurred that the Government had been right to curb unrestricted immigration and, in making this point, they stated that 'no one now really disputes the Government's right and duty to control immigration, if only for security reasons, and few would question the principle that Bahamians should be trained and preferred to fill all positions of employment wherever practicable'. The rub is in the qualification 'wherever practicable'. On the matter of finding Bahamian help or permitting expatriates to work in the Bahamas the Commission recommended that work permits be granted for the period it would take to train a Bahamian to fill the post (if none were available) and not an arbitrarily established period. The Commission reminded the Port Authority and its licensees of their contractual obligation 'to train Bahamian-born persons to fill positions of employment'. The Report proposed that the Port

Authority take the initiative and notes that certain (unnamed) licensees had 'agreed to contribute to a training and educational fund of approximately $1 million in the first year and $250,000 annually thereafter for a minimum of four years'. It suggested too that the Government might wish to offer scholarships for business management courses and for the professions, including chartered certified or public accountants, engineers, surveyors and others in which Bahamian-born persons are in short supply.

The Commission further reported that they were satisfied that the criminal activities of Freeport had been grossly exaggerated though they suggested ground rules for improving the security aspect of the island and they made a strong recommendation for the establishment of a prison. Housing, particularly for Bahamians, was discussed and the Commission made a recommendation that the Port Authority's obligation under the Amendment Agreement to build up to 800 low-cost houses be invoked assuming a clear demand for additional housing was justified. On agriculture, the Commission noted with horror that the bill for imports of foods into the island amounted to $47 million in 1970. Though not coming up with any specific blueprint for the type of strategy required, they suggested that all avenues possible be followed to explore the ways of increasing home production of produce and livestock.

As a conclusion, the Report states that Freeport stands as a monument to the vision, the optimism and industry of Mr Groves. It points out that the Government is not working to obstruct the development of Freeport, but only to change its direction. And to do this, dialogue is necessary which might be affected by the establishment of a 'forum' for an interchange of views between the Government and representatives of Freeport. (Interestingly, they made no mention of setting up a local authority.) In conclusion they stated that they wished to see Freeport not as '. . . a foreign outpost but as an integral part of the Bahamas community, carrying the Bahamian image, maintaining a Bahamian loyalty and promoting Bahamian security and uplifting the Bahamian economy'.

CHANGE OF GOVERNMENT

The Bahamas, and perhaps Grand Bahama in particular, stood at a crossroads in its history in the early seventies. It was suggested that development was being deliberately slowed down until Bahamians were able to participate in the business life of the country more fully themselves. But in fact there was clear evidence that in the comparatively few years since the signing of the Hawksbill Creek Agreement, the native sons of the island had undergone a quiet social and economic revolution indicating that they were already well entrenched in the economic mainstream. Progress would probably be more rapid if it had not been for the hemisphere-wide business recession.

In the next chapter we take a look at the background and lifestyle of the people of Grand Bahama in the context of their earlier and fast-disappearing island habitat.

9 SETTLEMENT AND SETTLERS

THE original land grants on Grand Bahama were made to absentee landlords who seldom visited the island and, as far as evidence suggests, did not attempt to settle there. They left their names to one or two communities like Hunter's and McLean's Town. After Emancipation, a certain amount of land was granted to former slaves though the more common practice was to occupy land and claim title afterwards. Possession of land to a Bahamian is almost a sacred trust. The importance he placed on ownership of the land often led him to build a stone wall around his property which demanded more effort than any house he might construct upon it. Some of the stone walls on the island were almost certainly built by slave labour since they encompass much larger areas than would be usual for individual ownership. These expertly coursed and fitted random rubble stone walls are the only physical evidence Grand Bahama possesses of the slave era.

The concept of acquiring land compatible with the intended building is quite foreign to most Bahamians. Frequently if a son marries he builds a house on the same parcel of land as his parents. If the cooking facilities are inadequate a separate building might be constructed with the 'open air' acting as a corridor between the two buildings. If the owner of the land suddenly became affluent the wooden structures may be demolished and a double-storey masonry house might be built in its place even though it might be surrounded by fairly mean shacks; and if the owner's interests are commercial, a shack might become a chicken coop, a barber's shop or a grocery store.

130

SETTLEMENT AND SETTLERS

The village settlements of Grand Bahama are the creation of Afro-Bahamian fortitude. They are built in the tradition of early European colonists but, since the economy of the out-islands did not permit the construction of large building complexes, they are quite simple, possessing a vernacular charm of their own. The basic requirement for a site selected for human habitation is the readily available supply of fresh water, so most villages were located on the 'mainland' near to a fresh-water source. Exceptions to this rule are Water Cay which was established on a small islet in the swashland of the north coast and the eastern settlements of McLean's Town and Sweeting's Cay which are similarly surrounded by salt water and have to supplement their ground water supply by cisterns.

With living near subsistence level there could be no question of an urban way of life. Instead the original inhabitants settled in a thin cluster of small houses mainly along the south coast. Paths were sometimes cut between the houses but most movement in early times was on foot along the beach which served as the principal highway. Often behind the dunes near to the settlements were scattered patches of cultivated land which to this day are planted with corn, sugar cane and vegetables and, on the fringe of the pine barren, citrus is sometimes grown. Provisions not obtainable on the island would be brought in by mail boat from Nassau which would moor off-shore at a few of the larger settlements. Fishing was the major source of livelihood and the fishermen's sloops and dinghies would be pulled up on the rocks above high water mark each day after use. An observer about two decades ago noted that ramps had been blasted out of rock in order to facilitate this task.

A typical village consisted of a few wooden-framed houses with a weather-boarded exterior, a cedar shingle roof, a small entrance verandah and shuttered windows. In the larger communities there was often a masonry church. The churches are the

131

oldest institution on the island. The Baptists who had a relatively large following built adequate but simple churches, one delightful example being the old church at Barbary Beach (near Peterson's Cay) constructed in 1901. This church is of masonry construction with walls rendered inside and out and roofed formerly with the customary shingles. When the community died out and the few young survivors moved elsewhere the church became a hermitage for Father Gerald Groves, a Trappist monk from the monastery of Gethsemany, Kentucky. Other Baptist churches are found in almost all the settlements, the more modern ones being impressively large but architecturally undistinguished. The Anglicans built a charming little church at Smith's Point (demolished in 1968); another one at Eight Mile Rock, named St Stephen, now considerably restored and enlarged; and at West End, where a picturesque little church, dedicated to St Mary Magdalene, was constructed in 1870.

The Roman Catholics were late in making a presence in Grand Bahama. However, in 1942 Monsignor Hawes, a 'hermit priest' of Cat Island and erstwhile architect, came out of voluntary seclusion and designed one or two churches for the Catholic diocese. In Hunter's he built a delightful barrel-vaulted church complete with belfry porch which was dedicated to St Vincent de Paul. The floor, as befits an orphan parish, is made up of tiles left over from the larger sister parishes of New Providence. In 1957 work started on a Roman Catholic church at West End but it was not until 1965 that St Michael's was finally completed and a priest was in residence. The same year work was begun on another Catholic church located at Seagrape and a year later a small defunct supermarket at High Rock was converted into a church and rectory.

In this century many fundamentalist religious communities have been established in the settlements of Grand Bahama: the Church of God of Prophecy has two very large churches, one at Eight Mile Rock and another at West End. The Seventh Day Adventists, Methodists, Church of God and Jehovah's Witnesses also built churches and have a large following. Tents of Revival churches, too, sprout up from time to time.

Freemasonry was introduced into the island in August 1950, when the Northern Star Lodge and Temple (African rite) moved to permanent headquarters in Seagrape with thirty members from West End and twenty-five from Eight Mile Rock. Other settlements have lodges of lesser-known orders which sometimes double as community centres. As a consequence of the Bahamian's abiding awareness of the mortality of man a burial society is to be found in almost every village.

SOCIO-CULTURAL BACKGROUND

The native Bahamians of the island are mainly of mixed European and African descent, the African element having originally been transported to the Bahamas as slaves from West Africa north of the Congo. The institution of slavery in the Caribbean can be traced back to the mid-seventeenth century when the Royal African Company more or less controlled the trade. It is of small consolation that slavery was never as cruel in the Bahamas as it was elsewhere, but even so it is revealing to note that not until 1774 was slave evidence admitted in the courts, only in 1807 were freed slaves allowed to vote and not until 1829 were slaves permitted to marry. The slave trade had been officially abolished by the British in 1807 and the Royal Navy maintained a special squadron to suppress the traffic. Several cargoes of freed slaves were taken to Nassau and there are records of one slaver being intercepted near Grand Bahama. Since the island by this time was inhabited it is possible that the astonished Africans were set free to make a new life for themselves on Grand Bahama. It took until 1834 for the Colonial legislature to make the final step to emancipate the slaves in the Bahamas. With the change in the economic structure that Emancipation brought, all Bahamians were to live a marginal existence with little differentiation between the richest and the poorest for the next century. Grand Bahamians were to live off the land and the sea, sometimes lumbering, occasionally sponging, but mostly fishing and farming until Butlin and Groves were to awaken the island out of its torpor in the post-World War II era.

All Bahamians savour their individualism, and this is nowhere better illustrated than in the Christian names they choose for themselves. Common or garden names are few indeed and instead parents endow their sons with such names as Horatio, Hurlbutt, Romulus and so on, and females answer to names like Cinderella, Willa-Mae and Evadne. Even nicknames are distinctive, for instance, a *maître d'hôtel* at a Freeport club known to all as 'Cochise' and a former strong-arm man at West End in the Prohibition Era called, with good reason, 'Shotgun John'. Surnames are mainly of Anglo-Saxon origin and derive from the days of slavery when the slaves took the same name as their overlord. There were so few families on Grand Bahama until recently that about a dozen or so surnames would encompass the great majority of the people. These family surnames include : Adderley, Bain, Bethell, Cooper, Hanna, Hepburn, Higgs, Johnson, Kemp, Laing, Lightbourn, Mather, Pinder, Russell, Smith, Taylor, Thomson, Wilchcombe, Williams. Indeed the close-knit nature of the early settlements needed special tact on the part of its inmates :

Islan' life ain' no fun less ya treat errybody
Like ya brudder, ya sister or ya frien'.
Love ya neighbour, play ya part, jes' remember das de art,
For when ocean fence ya in, all is kin.

The lumbering operation brought some new blood to the island from the rest of the Bahamas and the Turks and Caicos Islands. And later still the establishment of Freeport opened the floodgates to immigrants from all over the world.

Culturally the Grand Bahamian is typical of most out-islanders. He is resourceful, proud and God-fearing; if he has a fault it is his propensity to drink, a habit which extends to expatriates and tourists to the Bahamas alike. Reasons for the habit are not hard to find : climatically the Bahamas is a thirsty place, the merrymaking pervasive and alcoholic beverages are easily available, and relatively inexpensive. In fact Dr Richter, former Medical Officer for the Western District of Grand Bahama, isolated alcoholism as the most important medico-social problem. With so little to do in the settlements in earlier times Dr Richter concluded that drinking was one of the few ways of seeking solace from the monotony of everyday life. A health problem related to drinking is the extremely high incidence of cardio-vascular conditions often referred to by Bahamians as 'high blood'. Perhaps another social phenomenon which should be mentioned is the high rate of illegitimate births in the villages. In 1960 every one child in four was born out of wedlock though the number today appears to be falling. Despite what is conventionally considered to be a serious moral question there can be little doubt that the children so conceived are well cared for and satisfactory common law unions often ensue.

In speech Bahamians have a distinctive manner of expressing themselves which almost amounts to a separate dialect. Though a version of the Queen's English might be used when talking to an outsider, in conversation with his confreres the Bahamian often reverts to delightfully peculiar sentence structures and idioms. 'Went away' might be expressed as 'done gone'; according to a Bahamian song 'no money' is a 'pocket full o' empty' and 'a check' means a cold. A holdover from Elizabethan English (particularly noticeable in the speech of the Abaconians) is the irrational application of 'h' in front of words beginning with vowels and its omission from words actually beginning with an 'h'. But most pervasive is the substitution of 'v' for 'w' as in 'wision' (vision), 't' or 'd' for 'th' as in 'ting' (thing) or 'dey' (they). The apostrophe 's' of the genitive case is invariably absent so that Lucayan Beach (where Mr Groves has a house) is known as 'Mr Grove Beach', and to arrive at Freeport might be stated as 'he done reach Freeport' (the last word having equal emphasis on each syllable).

Bahamians are not particularly skilled at working with their hands though the women are good seamstresses. The men are exceptionally clothes-conscious and greatly influenced by the latest in modern, and sometimes African, fashion. But it is in their music and its associated dance movement that they particularly excel. Significantly the calypso, which was developed during the period of intense slavery in the West Indies, is not native in the Bahamas—instead a more melodic music form only faintly reminiscent of calypso has been developed. Goombay, as this form is called, provides a lilting tune and its lyrics tell of ordinary happenings and the commonplace surroundings of the Bahamians. Goombay has no dominant beat such as a chain gang might follow and there is hardly a word of social protest. Goombay rhythms tell of 'Brown skin girls' who mind the family while the breadwinner is away sailing, or, a popular debatable theme everywhere : 'men smart, women smarter'. During the governorship of the Duke of Windsor one sympathetic songwriter penned : 'it was love, love alone, that caused King Edward to leave the throne. . . '. Another famous Goombay song is by Blind Blake, perhaps the greatest exponent of this musical form, entitled 'Conch ain't got no bone', a charming little song about the shellfish which is a favourite dish of Bahamians. Musicians in the Bahamas invariably include Goombay music in their repertoire which often extends all the way from spirituals to the latest pop music. These rhythms serve as background music for dancing and feature such imports as the Ska, the Merengue, Rock Steady and more modern 'soul' music. In connection with the Goombay Summer Festival of 1971 a Grand Bahama musician, Jay Mitchell, wrote a popular promotional song which gained international acclaim called 'Goombay Summer in Freeport'. The last stanza describes the bazaar :

> Down to the bazaar you can get what your heart desire
> 'Cos it's Goombay Summer in Freeport, Freeport/Lucaya
> France, Spain, Africa, all places you want to go
> Between the Straw Market and the Casino
> We even got Mexico!
> 'Cos it's Goombay Summer in Freeport, Freeport/Lucaya !

Until recently the island was not without the sinister influence of Obeah and Voodoo, the latter being brought into the islands by the Haitian immigrants, though in the few cases recorded it has more to do with the extortion of money than evil spirits. Obeah is the more common form of 'witchcraft' practised in the Bahamas and it involves the working of harm by an Obeahman who is alleged to have particular magical powers over a person's enemies. Sometimes the Obeahman will invoke a spirit commonly referred to as a *duppie* obtained by going to a graveyard at night and digging up grave dirt. The spirit is then put upon the victim who can only free himself by the use of an even more potential counter-spell. Sometimes an Obeahman will make up a magic bundle and give it to his client to bury in the house or garden of the intended victim.

A frequently used Obeah 'spell' consists of hanging of bottles containing 'magic' potions on trees near to a cultivated area to keep trespassers away. Dr Richter cites an interesting incident involving Obeah in Grand Bahama in his 1960 Medical Report. It seems that in one of the eastern settlements a 21-year-old youth had a brain tumour and was sent to Nassau for treatment but he returned and died a few days later. The doctor was summoned to examine the body and when he arrived there he discovered the body already in a coffin surrounded by several hundred bystanders. On examining the body Dr Richter discovered two eggs and a fork in the coffin which he promptly removed. It seems that some of the people assembled thought that the youth died as the result of a *hex* or a curse and the eggs and fork, which had some part in his life in Nassau, were introduced as a counter-spell. After the doctor explained that medicine is not without its shortcomings and the death was from a tumour, the funeral proceeded without further incident. Obeah is often supposed to be employed by jealous wives or jilted lovers and sometimes the baby of a union is the intended victim as one letter shows :

Doctor I come down here (but) I was sick (and) some one was trying to hurt me (because of) my boyfriend and want to cross my baby in me, one day the baby been in my stomach but the midwife did some good for me; doctor I feel like I will die, please send me some after-pain pills and I will send the money on Tuesday. Thats why I did want you to send me to Nassau to have my baby because someone want to cross my baby, doctor I wish you could born him before time to save myself, you must ask no one for me because you wouldn't know the rite one.

Despite her fears a healthy baby was delivered and the psychosis vanished.

JUNKANOO

As if to remind the world of their African heritage, once a year, on Boxing Day (and sometimes at New Year), the islanders put on a Junkanoo parade. Junkanoo is a corruption of the name 'John Canoe' which, tradition suggests, belongs to a proud African chief who was brought into slavery in the Caribbean. It is thought that since he was accustomed to a very different life-style in Africa, at Christmas when his overlords were preoccupied with themselves he re-enacted his former state by dressing himself up in whatever bright bits and pieces he could find and, with his entourage following suit, they put on a grand parade. Another theory suggests that the word stems from the French phrase *gens inconnus* (the unknown people), unknown because they are disguised by the fanciful masks that always accompany their outlandish costumes. Another plausible explanation is based on the French *jeunes caneurs*, the name of the young field hands who worked in the sugar cane plantations of Haiti and other Caribbean islands. Junkanoo can be traced back to Jamaica as early as 1801 but by the mid-nineteenth century there were reports in Nassau of 'John Canoe' parades in the Bahamas. The parade starts at dawn when groups of people in crepe paper costumes, sometimes following a theme, sometimes not, march through the streets to the accompaniments of drums, whistles and cow bells. To set the marching pace, whistles, bugles and, more recently, steel drums are used to provide a tune of sorts. The parade has an almost hypnotic effect on participants and bystanders alike.

The best known Junkanoo is held in Nassau though smaller parades are held in the larger settlements in the out-islands. In Grand Bahama the Junkanoo procession at West End is perhaps the most authentic, though the parade in Freeport promises to surpass it in popularity. Nowadays Junkanoo features sponsored groups and 'floats' and much secrecy and competition between rival participants, and often prizes are even awarded for the best entries. However, despite the influence of commercialism, Junkanoo remains the premier cultural expression of the Bahamian.

ADMINISTRATION

The local administration of the island since the mid-nineteenth century has been by out-island commissioners until recently appointed by the governor. The first commissioners resided at Golden Grove on the south coast which was probably chosen because it was about the geographical centre of the island. The function of a commissioner in the Colonial Civil Service made him the most important administrative officer of government at local level. Generally a justice of the peace, the commissioner was in charge of the police, public works, education and health, as well as the dispensation of justice. Under the colonial administrative system the governor set the standard of government for the colony, so the commissioner set the standard of local administration. In the early days political representation was invariably by an absentee Nassau merchant whose constituency until very recently also included the island of Bimini. The first native son to represent the island was Warren Levarity, a resident of West End who was elected to the House in 1960 as the Progressive Liberal Party candidate; later Harold DeGregory of West End and Maurice Moore of Pinder's Point (PLP) were elected as the people's representatives.

To give voice to the communities of the island the Grand Bahama Citizens Committee was formed in the early 1960s. With representatives from the principal settlements of the island the Committee convened every month or so to discuss matters of mutual interest. Recommendations of the Committee were passed on to the Government by way of the local member of the House. Though serving as an important forum for matters concerning the island, the deliberations of the Committee were in private and, having no executive power, its motions were susceptible to being ignored.

SOCIETY IN TRANSITION

The churches have provided an important stabilising influence through the period of rapid social transition. The development of Freeport has had the effect of creating a dualistic society on the island and although there has been no overt friction and surprisingly little labour unrest, the native Bahamians, together with other West Indians, generally do not mix with the white population except at work. Background, education and mutual apprehension have the effect of keeping the races apart and there have been few, if any, institutions which permit and encourage socialising, though this is slowly changing.

Just as the white element is not homogeneous, being composed of white Bahamians, English, Americans, Poles, etc., so the black element is similarly culturally fractionalised. French-speaking Haitians tend to occupy the lowest rung on the social ladder, many of them being political refugees, though a great majority are in the Bahamas for the job opportunities. Since they are uncertain newcomers, they perform their work efficiently in more menial tasks. Other West Indians generally find themselves in a better position owing to their common language and generally better educational background. Many English-speaking West Indians are employed in tertiary occupations as secretaries, clerks and professionals.

The Grand Bahamian has remained in his native settlement

unless he sold out to the developers in the early days and was thus impelled to move on. As the people who lease accommodation in the settlements improve their financial status, they tend to move to the better housing accommodation of Freeport, some of which has 'filtered down' from the pioneer families who have recently moved elsewhere. But as one moves further away from Freeport, so the settlements are culturally and physically less affected.

There is no question that without the hard work, adaptability and patience of the native Bahamians and other West Indian migrants the Freeport miracle could not have been achieved. Every day many hundreds of Bahamians and West Indians travel to Freeport from the settlements to work in the hotels, on construction sites, banks, offices and shops. In the space of ten years many of the indigenous Bahamians have adjusted from being subsistence farmers and fishermen, some with little or no formal education, to highly respected and productive members of an urban community. Others found their careers in the world of business, politics and education. Of the latter group one of the best-known Grand Bahamians is Susan Wallace (née Bethel) who, though she now resides in Nassau, recently wrote a charming book of poetry *Bahamian Scene*, which includes some reminiscences of her childhood in West End in a delightful poem entitled 'The place where I was born' and other verses quoted in this book.

The island's new-found affluence and its concomitant evolution may have caused many Bahamians to desert their former lifestyle but fortunately not their distinctive Bahamian identity.

10   PLANNING OF FREEPORT/ LUCAYA

THE Hawksbill Creek Agreement was drafted with the idea of establishing an industrial community on Grand Bahama. In its reference to the delegation of responsibility for planning, the Agreement is brief and succinct: clause 2 sub-clause (22) states in part: 'The Port Authority shall have the sole right . . . to plan, lay out and vary the development of the Port Area in such a manner as the Port Authority shall in their absolute discretion deem fit and proper. . . .' Thus the Port Authority had a clear mandate to plan the 200-odd square miles designated by the Government as the 'Port area'.

Early planning looked to an industrial zone around the harbour and a residential area to the east replacing the settlement at Pine Ridge which was being phased out. Later it was decided, with the understandable arbitrariness that typified the early development of Freeport, to create a residential settlement in the pine barren about five miles east of the harbour. The man responsible for the early planning was Jan Porel (a ward of the Pierpont Morgan family) who had already excelled as a grand opera singer, surveyor and engineer, and incidentally was the project manager of the Oak Ridge Atomic Center in Tennessee. His original plan proposed the building of a dual mall running north and south with a commercial zone between and residential subdivisions either side. The first housing was makeshift and was constructed to the west of the Mall in 1957 and became known as Silver City, or, by its detractors, 'Tin City' (after the metal siding used in its construction) and a corresponding settlement was started shortly thereafter in the east, called Marco City. For

142

Page 143 Shopping: (above) street in the Spanish section of the bazaar, Freeport; (below) Churchill Square, Freeport. The inscription under the huge Churchill bust reads: 'If we pick a quarrel between the past and the present, we shall find that we have lost the future'

Page 144 (right) The most interesting land animal on the island: *Leicephalus Carinatus Armouri* or curly-tailed lizard; *(below)* Bell-shaped 'boiling' hole about half-a-mile inland from 'Old' Freetown. Holes like this are linked with the sea by underground channels

the few who could afford it, higher-priced land was reserved for housing on a low ridge near the sea; the name of these 'sub-divisions' invoked for the first time the Indian heritage of the islands, the areas being called respectively: Lucayan Ridge (elevation 50ft!) and Lucayan Beach.

The choice of the name 'Lucaya' would have gratified R. A. Curry, a Bahamian man of letters, who wrote in 1928: 'Indeed it would be a pity were this name to become entirely lost. It might well be substituted for a name of some island which has no special meaning and thus be preserved on the Bahamian maps, but also be written on all maps of the world.' (In fact if the plans for the Port area are put into effect Lucaya could shortly become the largest settlement in the Bahamas.) A requirement of the early development was the need for low-cost housing (particularly for imported labour from other islands) and this was constructed south of Silver City and became known colloquially as 'West Side Village'. Land was reserved for industry between West Side Village and the harbour. The only road at this time was the former right of way of the Pine Ridge railway (now Queen's Highway) and nearly all the early business spread out along this unpaved thoroughfare. The theory was to develop an industrial continuum from east to west starting with service and light industries and terminating with heavy and extractive industries around the harbour. However, lack of developers in those early days rendered the theory largely academic. A few years after the signing of the Agreement the promising Bahamas Shipyards venture fizzled out and Mr Ludwig, not surprisingly, continued to have his ships built in Japan. But Freeport was left with a commodious harbour—all that was needed was the commerce to justify it.

The year 1958 witnessed the establishment of the Freeport Bunkering Company, which occupied a 40 acre site some 400yd east of the harbour; later the Bahama Cement Company constructed a plant on the west side of the harbour and built a housing compound for the imported help. The cement company subsequently bought the area known as 'Silver City' and demolished the temporary buildings. They also purchased about 1,400 acres of land north of the harbour which will be surface-mined for limestone. Their long-term plan also calls for dredging Hawksbill Creek to obtain more limerock and, in so doing, they will almost double the size of the present harbour. The output of the cement plant in 1970 was 900,000 tons.

In 1960 the Freeport area was studied by the students of the City Planning Department of Cornell University, and in October of the same year they published a report entitled *Freeport—Lucayan Town*. Their study, though never adopted officially, virtually became the master plan for Freeport. The report consisted of four parts: Administration and historical background; Social-economic considerations; Philosophy and group studies; and Regional plan. In the report it is the group studies which are most interesting from a planning viewpoint. Group One decided upon a lineal development, placing Freeport almost exactly where it is today, locating a university town in the Peterson's Cay area and placing a series of 'agricultural towns' where Lucaya Estates has been laid out. Group Two focused on tourism; industry is retained in the west with beach-front hotel and resort sites on the south coast with residential lots inland. A waterway bisecting the island was proposed in the exact location of the present Grand Lucayan Waterway. Another group used the word 'playground' to convey their concept. Taking note from the traditional Caribbean settlements, they built the city around the harbour. But though they calculated an ultimate population of 200,000 they did not carry their planning beyond the present centre of Freeport and they made Hawksbill Creek the focus of all the proposed development.

In the final scheme the groups combined and a regional plan was prepared. The result was a little disappointing. The idea of the through-island canal was not carried forward and a low-density residential belt was proposed stretching from the town centre eastwards for thirty miles. A section was inserted on the aged population purporting to suggest that there might be considerable numbers of North Americans who might choose to reside on the island after retirement (due to the high cost of living no such desire has yet been manifest). However, the students were almost exactly correct in predicting a yearly flow of 400,000 tourists within ten years and they cited the projection made by the Cornell Hotel School, that this tourist population would need about six 18-hole golf courses. (In 1971 the tourist figure was over 500,000 and there were five 18-hole golf courses in operation.) Other proposals were the establishment of a cement plant on the island and the creation of an industrial park which, twelve years after the signing of the Hawksbill Creek Agreement, has been realised by the construction of the Freeport Industrial Park. Recreational and community facilities, including an underwater park, were also suggested. Finally a less realistic suggestion was the adoption of the Scottish system of local government for the 'burghs' with bailies and bailiwicks! (Freeport has yet to obtain local government.) However, with the advantage of hindsight in appraising the Cornell Report, one must say that many of their ideas were prophetic.

In an attempt to promote industry to the island Jan Porel prepared a schematic proposal for an aircraft maintenance and service area in what is today the county area of Lucaya. This farsighted concept anticipated the need for training facilities in the region preceding by some ten years the controversial Dade County jetport proposed for the Everglades in Florida. The idea was presented to the airlines to study but an important development overtook the proposal. The turning-point in the history and consequently the planning of Freeport was the year 1960, when the Supplemental Agreement was signed permitting the Port Authority to expand into tourism and residential development.

As a result of this new Agreement the Grand Bahama Development Company was created for the purpose of developing and selling 100,000 acres of land to be known as Lucaya. The Development Company also contracted to construct the 200-room luxury hotel before 31 December 1963 called for in the Agreement. Shortly thereafter the Development Company signed a contract with Taylor International to plan the 108,332 acre residential tract and sometime later they took a full page in a local newspaper to state 'we are working on plans for our area, which we hope will soon be ready'. The 18,000 acres already partly developed at the western end of the Port area and still owned by the Port Authority was known as the 'Industrial Service Area' and, as its name suggests, was to become the industrial hub of the community. To enforce development in the Freeport 'Service area' the Port Authority sold residential land at a little below market value but held the deeds to the property in escrow until the land had been built upon. This single factor had the profound effect of encouraging building which in turn acted like a catalyst on the development cycle. This condition was to cause the rapid physical development of Freeport while resort use and residential land in Lucaya was sold primarily for speculation purposes. Most of the development in the early 1960s took place in the so-called East Sections of Freeport (or that area east of the Malls). A few detached houses were built, but in the main the hybrid 'duplex' (a semi-detached bungalow) and scores of small apartment buildings were constructed. But despite the architectural mediocrity of these early buildings, they served a vital need.

In the months that followed, Taylor International prepared subdivision layouts and a master plan for the Lucaya area. The through-island canal idea was resurrected, a University City (located near the waterway) was planned, a series of south coast 'community centres' were shown and a continuous inland waterway parallel to the south coast which would create valuable property out of the swashland near the beach was suggested. This latter proposal resulted in the construction of Bell Channel Bay adjacent to the proposed site for the luxury hotel, which was later named the Lucayan Beach Hotel. An 18-hole championship golf course was projected north of Bell Channel and a well-known American golf course architect was commissioned to prepare the design. At the same time, privately-sponsored canal developments were under construction at Bahama Terrace south of Freeport proper and on a small cay renamed Queen's Cove to the northwest of Freeport, which had been bought by the Mary Carter

148

Paint Company (the same company which developed Paradise Island, Nassau). Another private developer, Grand Bahamian Hills Ltd, purchased 400 acres of rolling pine land west of the Lucayan Ridge and subdivided it into $\frac{1}{3}$-acre single-family residential lots. By mid-1962 Taylor International had prepared an aerial perspective showing the proposed curvilinear form of street layout intended for Lucaya. However, six months later, due to Taylor's financial difficulties, their contract was terminated.

In December 1962 the Development Company announced that they were organising their own engineering and construction department—the planning function seems to have been temporarily overlooked—and it remained that way until early 1964 when Harland Bartholomew, an American planning firm, was retained by the Development Company to prepare a master plan of the Lucaya area. A year later the Port Authority set up its own planning department. With the burgeoning growth that the Port area experienced after 1960, it became obvious that an updated master plan of development was not only necessary, but imperative. Accordingly, a 'Generalised Land Use Plan' was prepared showing in outline the most desirable pattern of growth, taking into account the existing construction, possible future land use and developmental economics. This interim plan was recognised as a necessary guide to orderly future growth of the community but it was broad enough to accommodate adjustment to new industrial and tourist needs in addition to being sensitive to possible changes in patterns of living.

This same year D. K. Ludwig reappeared on the scene. In a joint agreement Mr Ludwig and the Port Authority proposed to develop a 1,000 acre tract of land for residential and hotel use around another 18-hole championship golf course. They further agreed to create a shopping centre for tourists and a new company, Bahamas Amusements Ltd, decided to build a new casino nearby. The joint venture was short lived, however, and Mr Ludwig opted for the building of a hotel and the development of 'Bahamia', an exclusive residential estate built around the golf course. The King's Inn, as the hotel was called, is currently the largest in the Bahamas with 800 rooms and later, in 1970, when the 400-room, 12-storey International Hotel was constructed on a nearby site it became the largest resort complex in the Caribbean area. To enhance the appearance of his investment Mr Ludwig established a nursery which aided in preserving natural vegetation and subsequent replanting of the entire tract of land. From the corporate 'divorce' the Port Authority obtained custody of the half-finished buildings known as the International Bazaar which were transformed under the expert direction of a Hollywood set designer and decorator into various national sections each having an architectural character appropriate to the geographic area it represented. Unquestionably the idea of creating an *olde worlde* environment in a modern new town is incongruous, yet nevertheless the completed Bazaar has a charm and authenticity that has converted most of the former cynics.

Meanwhile the central area of Freeport was developing apace. A new supermarket and some single-storey commercial buildings were constructed in the interim period after Jan Porel retired and before the planning department was created. Eventually a downtown square with a parade ground and landscaping was provided with an avenue of trees terminating in a larger than life-size bronze head portrait of Sir Winston Churchill, by sculptor Marshall Fredericks. The town centre, however is not without its critics; Mary Slater, the author of *The Caribbean Islands*, writes: 'Downtown Freeport is functional, there is an utter lack of anything even verging on the beautiful, amid brash newness is a certain brave pioneering atmosphere which has to be appreciated if it cannot be admired. . . . This is a place of the future, the chosen home for settlers of today and tomorrow. It can never be a typical out-island' (but then, the developers might add, it was never intended to be!).

Elsewhere two other major real estate developments were taking shape. A company known as Bahama Reef and Country Club acquired 466 acres of land west of Bell Channel from the Development Company and started constructing an 18-hole golf course and (inevitably) some canals. Tamarind Development

Company similarly acquired land for another canal development known as Fortune Bay and developed residential land around another golf course. The broadening of the economic base to include tourism added a great stimulus not only from the cash flow associated with resort facilities, but also from the vast programme of land sales in the low-density residential area of Lucaya and so not unnaturally interest in land speculation and the new resort facilities caused industry to give Freeport a second look. The result was a vast expansion in the number and diversity of licences issued by the Port Authority which further aided the growth spiral. Due to the high cost of buying and preparing the land for cultivation, one market gardener successfully resorted to hydroponic farming. This gravel-culture operation provides a yield of fruit and vegetables on one-tenth of the land necessary for conventional farming. Indeed estimates show that the 15 acre hydroponic farm could yield up to one million pounds of vegetables per year.

In order to address itself to the many needs of the working population a low-cost housing project, called for in the Amendment Agreement of 1966, was started on land north of the settlement of Hunter's. Two hundred single-family houses were built with mortgage loans insured under the Bahamas Housing Act and a small commercial centre was started. The future plans call for the construction of another 800 dwelling houses, an enlarged commercial area, and other community buildings. From 1964 to 1970 development was extremely rapid. The Development Company through their sales agents, Intercontinental Realty, sold residential lots in the Lucaya area to expatriate investors at a phenomenal rate. The preliminary master plan of the Lucaya area was followed, perhaps too strictly, in the ensuing demand for land. Though the through-island canal became a reality with the construction of the Grand Lucayan Waterway, the idea of 'communities' was not adopted, making the Lucaya area virtually a dormitory area reliant on the service industrial facilities of Freeport (though this may be changed in the future by the establishment of a new industrial zone at the eastern end of the island).

A study of the economic effects of the early planning decisions reveals a paradox. The least valuable land has been made into the highest priced real estate; for example, the cay in Hawksbill Creek, re-named Queen's Cove, which was once only attainable by an inconvenient dinghy trip through a mangrove swamp, today features land prices which range from $10,000 to $40,000 an acre; the former pine barren land where the central area of Freeport is now situated (making it the only inland city of the Bahamas) sells for up to $80,000 an acre. Bell Channel, which was once swashland, is almost sold out and resales fetch up to $100,000 an acre depending on location, and the Grand Lucayan Water-way—which was once a mosquito-infested through-island slough —markets at prices ranging from $40,000 to $65,000 an acre. Though most land was sold as a 'hedge' against inflation some land in now developed areas has appreciated in five years to values treble its original price! And in 1971, in an attempt to maintain a cash flow, a new scheme known as the 'Preferred Investors Programme' offered customers in the Lucaya area the opportunity to trade their holdings for property of greater value. In so doing the purchaser received credit on the new purchase of the appreciated value from his original contract.

Looking back we might review the planning of Freeport/Lucaya over the past fifteen years. Despite, or perhaps because of, the lack of restraints the new community is not a Utopia. Some bizarre crimes more often associated with large cities are occasionally committed; there are an alarming number of traffic accidents for the size of the population and alcoholism is on the increase. On the other hand religious and charitable organisa-tions abound as witnessed by the number of churches, associations, societies and guilds in Freeport. The emphasis on the encourage-ment of development at all costs has not prompted a very high standard of architectural design, though all buildings constructed are structurally sound due to the rigidly enforced Building Code. As evidenced by Freeport it is clear that for other new town projects to be successful there must be great impetus right from the start of development. The components which make up a town like schools, shops, housing and factories must be so phased that they are completed almost simultaneously since all are needed at the same time. Where this strategy is not employed even the best proposals run the danger of being stillborn. Many highly publicised projects in the Bahamas and elsewhere have failed to materialise because there was not a simultaneous fusion of investors, capital, entrepreneurs and people.

Freeport/Lucaya has been hailed as a kind of 'miracle new town' and it is, certainly by Caribbean standards, exceptionally commodious, clean and functional and it provides an interesting model for new town development by private enterprise in the Caribbean context. Most of the negative features of the planning of Freeport/Lucaya are happily remediable. Perhaps not enough has been done to correct the minor but obvious faults of the original master plan where suburbia threatens to extend unrelieved for miles, few town-size community centres have been planned and so far only a few acres have been devoted for a second industrial zone. Natural sand dunes have been removed to the possible detriment of flood control and everywhere vegetation is demolished by bulldozers in the name of progress. Unhappily, typical of the mid-twentieth century, there is even some beach pollution by tankers and a hint of air pollution by the factories and industrial plants. The growth of Freeport far exceeds the original expectations with the result that sprawling single-storey buildings in the central area are now incompatible for the size of the city. There is a dire need for a link with the sea to enforce visually Freeport's role as a maritime community—and since universal detached single-family housing is economically impossible there is a great need for more compact, better designed, multi-family dwellings. Above all the new construction must be compatible with the Bahamian environment, especially in the paramount need for more landscaping in developed areas. To this end the Port Authority and the Development Company carried out a half million dollar landscaping programme in 1970.

Sir Thomas More, who perhaps had more than just a political idea to express, clearly saw his Utopia as a place where housing and landscaping were seriously considered. He writes that three-storey houses 'each of which has a storey projecting over the one below [a modern form much in vogue now] built in rows without any separation' (he seems here to be describing terrace housing or what in the United States are sometimes called 'garden apartments') and landscaping would be provided, 'for Utopians . . . set great store by their gardens'. However, he anticipates the suburban mentality when he writes : 'I needs confess and grant many things be in the Utopian weal-public that in our cities I may rather wish than hope for.' Freeport may not be a Utopia but nevertheless it stands as a significant example of community planning by private enterprise.

THE population growth of Grand Bahama in recent years has been directly related to the emergence of Freeport as the second city of the Bahamas. The marked acceleration in growth is due mainly to people from outside the Bahamas taking up residence in Freeport and Lucaya. From the tremendously thorough records kept by Dr Richter, one is able to obtain information on the population composition of the island as well as its medical history. In his 1969 report he noted that not only would the Bahamian have been outnumbered by expatriate whites, but within a decade Haitians would have outnumbered Bahamians on the island (the recent immigration policy has subsequently reversed this trend). In 1967 the settlements of West End, Eight Mile Rock and Pinder's Point were a little under 50 per cent Haitian in composition and the total of Haitians on the island at this time was estimated by Dr Richter as 5,320 compared with 17,680 Bahamians.

The most recent census of the Commonwealth of the Bahama Islands was taken in April 1970 and it records that at that time there were 168,833 people in the Bahamas, of whom about 26,043 (or about 15 per cent) were resident in Grand Bahama. Of these 13,679 were male and 12,364 were female. This preponderance of males is typical of developing areas. In fact, of the eighteen populated islands recorded in the census only three others, all islands on which major development is taking place (Abaco, Berry Island and Bimini), recorded more males than females. It should be noted, however, that illegal immigrants did not respond to the census and others were not available for questioning or refused to co-operate with the census-takers so the figures are

155

certainly on the low side. The population growth of the island shown against the background of important events in the life of the nation is shown on the Population Graph below.

Since this census was taken the island has lost some of its population particularly in the expatriate sector. The last can be explained in part by the programme of Bahamianisation and partly by the economic recession of the early 1970s which forced

POPULATION GROWTH OF GRAND BAHAMA

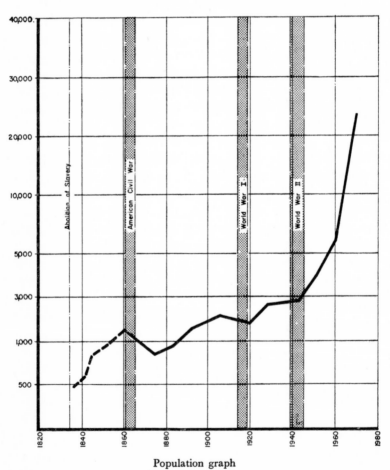

Population graph

migrants back to their point of origin. *The Manpower Utilisation Survey* of 1968 pointed out that Freeport had a predominantly foreign workforce.

In contrast to New Providence it was shown that there were no occupations in Freeport in which Bahamians and Belongers occupied more than 50 per cent of the total employment. In business services, 50 per cent of the employees were expatriates, 28 per cent residents and 12 per cent Bahamians and Haitians. In commerce and business there were 50 per cent expatriates, 8·3 per cent residents and 38 per cent Bahamians and Belongers. In addition, a large number of expatriates were found in community services, manufacturing and recreational services.

Construction was noted as one of the sectors in which there were more Bahamians than expatriates, namely 40 per cent Bahamians and Belongers, 21 per cent residents, 20 per cent expatriates, 11 per cent Haitians—but even here, numerically the number of expatriates was more than 1,000.

An occupational breakdown in Freeport showed further that expatriates filled the largest number of occupations of the professional and technical type plus the managerial and executive ones. While 60 per cent and 64 per cent respectively were expatriates in these sectors, Bahamians and Belongers comprised only 11 per cent and 14 per cent respectively. It is also noteworthy that 'residents' filled more of these high level positions than Bahamians, being 23 per cent in the first instance and 22 per cent in the second.

A table in this same report showed the above position even more graphically.

Bahama Islands: Percentage distribution of employees in establishments with five or more workers in each area by nationality (1st quarter 1968)

	Total	Bahamians and Belongers	Non-Bahamian Residents	Haitians	Expatriates
Total	100·0	69·0	6·2	6·8	18·0
New Providence	100·0	83·7	2·5	3·1	10·7
Freeport	100·0	34·1	15·6	13·0	37·3
Other Out-islands	100·0	64·9	5·6	13·3	16·2

GRAND BAHAMA

This table clearly paints a picture of foreign involvement, if not domination, in Freeport, which Government policy set out to change.

The growth in tourism has been phenomenal. In 1960 about 40,000 tourists visited Grand Bahama. In 1970 the figure was over ½ million, which is more than visited Jamaica the same year, and represents about 40 per cent of the Bahamas total. This increase in tourism to an 'out-island' is one of the outstanding events in the recent history of the Bahamas. The meteoric growth of Grand Bahama as a tourist resort in fact prompted the Ministry of Tourism to make special reference to the island in its advertising campaign by using the caption: 'Nassau, *Grand Bahama* and the Out Islands'. The island in 1970 had just under 4,000 hotel bedrooms which were principally located in Freeport and Lucaya

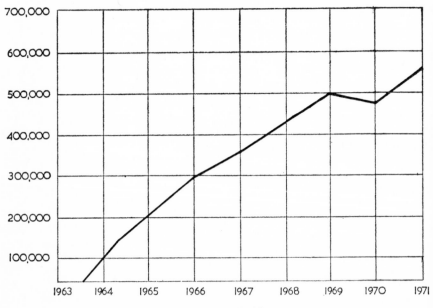

Annual number of visitors

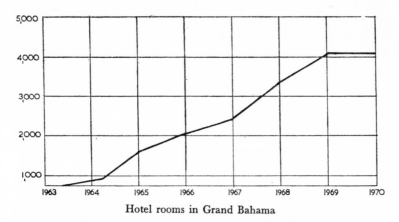

Hotel rooms in Grand Bahama

though there were hotels in West End, Eight Mile Rock, and Deep Water and Sweeting's Cays. The standard of accommodation ranged between the *de luxe* Lucayan Beach Hotel to the chalet-type cottages of the east end and the strangely named Take-me Hotel of Eight Mile Rock. The seaside Grand Bahama Hotel at West End, because of its self-contained nature, has the greatest variety of tourist facilities. The other resort hotels are either situated on the ocean-front, the island waterways or near the centre of Freeport. The normal mode of accommodation is with a room and two meals per day (Modified American Plan). Almost all hotels boast a dining-room, sometimes a separate coffee shop and invariably a cocktail bar. There are several good restaurants, the best of which are in the casinos and the International Bazaar.

To underline the importance of tourism we need only look at the tourism expenditure in the Bahamas. In 1969 the Ministry of Tourism estimated that $235 million was spent in the Bahamas by tourists, which, by apportionment, would suggest that about $90 million (40 per cent) was spent in Grand Bahama the same year.

Grand Bahama has several features, both natural and man-made, which make it an ideal tourist venue. The year-round mild climate, which is particularly pleasant between November and

159

May (the busiest months), beckons visitors from the frigid north. Then nature has endowed the Bahamas with exceptionally clear waters which, together with the fine white powder sand of the shoreline, make the beaches in the Bahamas amongst the best in the world; and fishing, scuba diving and boating are superb in the waters around the island. In an island that thrives on superlatives, visitors may cruise on the 'World's largest glass bottomed boat' and see, from the comfort of a deck chair, the beautiful underwater world of the reefs. Of the man-made attributes, the casino has had an undoubted magnetism which has drawn tourists who were looking for more than could be found on the other 700 similarly endowed islands.

Communications

The increase in tourism would not have been possible without a highly efficient transportation system. Sea transportation to and from West End and Freeport harbours has played a major role in providing building materials, food and other goods so necessary for servicing the developing community. But besides the cargo handled by the harbours about 32 per cent of all tourists visiting the island arrived by sea (1971). The MV *Grand Bahama* and the MV *Freeport*, which mainly operate as ferries to and from the mainland, bring many visitors to the island though cruise ships are increasing the number of calls they make at Freeport. The old faithful mailboat, too, still makes regular trips to Nassau from Sweeting's Cay, Freeport and West End. Besides the deep-water harbours, there are also useful harbours for shallow-draught boats at Gold Rock Creek, North Riding Point and McLean's Town.

Most visitors to the island, however, arrive by air through both the Freeport and the West End gateways. Air Canada, British Overseas Airways Corporation, Eastern, Northeast Airlines and Pan American Airways provide the island with an airlink to Miami. Smaller carriers like Shawnee and Mackey Airlines serve Boston, Toronto, London, Mexico, Jamaica, New York and several points in Florida and Flamingo, and Out Island Airways provide frequent daily services to and from Nassau. Without question had it not been for timely inauguration of services by these airlines the tourist development of the island would have been seriously hampered. Indeed there are few communities in the world with such a small permanent population that can boast such a comprehensive schedule of air services. The island has three jet strips and two unpaved runways suitable for light planes (Deep Water Cay and North Riding Point).

The surface transportation on the island is exclusively by motor vehicle. The powerful taxi union has effectively monopolised the movement of passengers. A few buses operate on a jitney basis with standard routes, but seldom to a fixed timetable. For sightseeing some ancient London double-decker buses found a new lease of life in Freeport, though their movement is strictly confined to the Port area. Freeport probably has the best road system in the Caribbean with the phenomenon of a surplus of roads in new but undeveloped subdivisions.

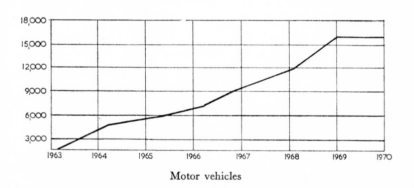

Motor vehicles

Communications on the island are good. From the primitive hand-cranked telephone system of the early days of the Hawksbill Creek Agreement, the Freeport area had three exchanges and 13,319 telephones in service in 1970. Long distance telephone service in the Bahamas is the responsibility of the Bahamas Telecommunications Corporation (a Government-owned company). Utilising the forward-scatter system there are telecommunication

K

facilities in West End, Freeport, Water Cay, Sweeting's Cay and High Rock which give excellent service to all parts of the world. In 1972 a submarine cable was laid to link the island with the mainland and direct long distance dialling followed shortly thereafter.

Fair television reception can be obtained by aerial from Florida (the Bahamas do not yet have a television network) but better reception is obtained by connection to the Community Antenna Cable Television service (CATV) which serves the whole of the developed area of Freeport. The Government-owned radio station ZNS provides a good signal to Grand Bahama and, besides the entertainment value of the station, ZNS provides an important function to out-islanders in broadcasting shipping notices, weather and tidal information and notices of births, marriages, deaths and so on. All two-way communications media keep in touch with the Bahamas Air Sea Rescue Association (BASRA) when emergencies occur. BASRA, which is a non-profit organisation, fulfils a vital lifesaving role in and around the historically dangerous waters of the Bahama Islands.

Presumably because of the scattered nature of settlements in the Bahamas there is no postal delivery service. Instead all mail is left in *poste restante* boxes at Government-owned postal agencies in the larger settlements. In cases where there are no postal boxes, letters should be addressed for 'general delivery'.

COMMERCE AND INDUSTRY

In the rapid development which the island has experienced over the last ten years, commerce and industry have been well out in front. The major industrial enterprises have been noted previously but the number and variety of small businesses which were established on the island, gambling on a high rate of growth from a low base, is remarkable. At 1 January 1971 there were about 550 investor-builders who were not very active at that time on account of the slump in the building industry, but most of the others, excluding some bankruptcies, continued to operate profitable businesses—though few sustained the high profit margin of the boom years. Because of the provisions of the Hawksbill Creek Agreement most of the commercial and industrial activity has been restricted to Freeport.

Licences to operate businesses are issued by the Port Authority to applicants who provide evidence of competence in the field for which the application is made, and who also prove that they have the capital and skills required to pursue such business. After the licence has been confirmed by Government the licensee may establish premises in Freeport. The term of the licence varies but most are for the duration of the Hawksbill Creek Agreement. Individuals or companies licensed by the Port Authority pay a fee generally commensurate with the annual gross receipts of their business. Indicative, perhaps, of the capital-hungry nature of development, the island has over a dozen branches of banks of international standing.

In the early years of Freeport an industrial commission was established to encourage industry but it was not very active. The industrial growth of Freeport in fact has been more indebted to the Adam Smith concept of the 'invisible hand', since investors of all sorts were imperceptibly motivated to establish businesses in Freeport. To illustrate the range of firms which located in Freeport one might list the cement plant, the oil refinery, Syntex Corporation (the oral contraceptive manufacturer) at one end of the scale and ballet teachers, manicurists, and numismatists at the other. In fact investment on the island has given Grand Bahama a solid economic base and an impressive industrial infrastructure. The investors have come from mainly North America and Europe and have provided the island with a very favourable basic/service industrial ratio. This ratio used by urban economists compares the industries earning foreign currency (basic) to those industries which derive their revenue from the local population (service). In short, this means that the local economy can sustain growth when it is being replenished from outside and thus avoid the stagnating effect of 'taking in each other's washing'. The unhealthy side effect of the foreign investment and the lack

163

of natural resources in the Bahamas, however, has been a high rate of inflation and high cost of living which increased at a greater rate than even the United States. According to the Bahamas Department of Statistics the Retail Price Index for all items rose from 100 on 1 January 1966 to 129 on 1 January 1970.

Economic activity outside of Freeport is concentrated mainly at the hotel at West End, the few commercial establishments of Eight Mile Rock (of which the Friendship Shopping Centre is the chief) and Pinder's Point and the Missile Base. Elsewhere farming and fishing help supplement income but most wage earners commute to Freeport for their principal source of income. The main sources of independent enterprise amongst Grand Bahamians are straw work (which is sold in the Bazaar and at most hotels), the ownership of taxis and buses, shops and bars. Bahamians mainly from Nassau have established as wine and spirit merchants, dry cleaners, wholesale food and building material suppliers and caterers, and a great many others are in the entertainment business.

The industrial infra-structure in the form of airports, harbours and communications is among the best in the Caribbean and it has the added advantage of being brand new. Energy is derived

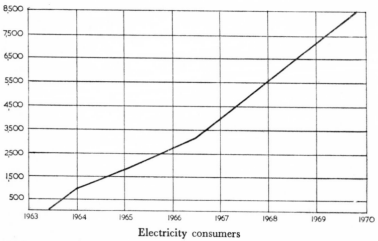

Electricity consumers

mainly from oil and electricity. By 1971 Grand Bahama had an installed electric generating capacity of 120,000 megawatts which was the second greatest single source of power in the whole of the Bahamas. The island has also natural water resources to support at least half a million people, and by supplementing the ground water with desalinised water, Grand Bahama could ultimately support even more.

POLITICS AND GOVERNMENT

The need for political reform was felt early in Grand Bahama. In 1960 Warren Levarity (Progressive Liberal Party) was elected to the House of Assembly, representing the Grand Bahama and Bimini district, though in November 1962, after the first election conducted on a universal franchise, the seat was lost to the United Bahamian Party. Before the historic election of 1967 two constituencies had been created on Grand Bahama, both of which were easily won by the Progressive Liberal Party. After the contention between the Port Authority licensees and the Government over the Hawksbill Creek Agreement, a rift appeared in the Progressive Liberal Party. The Minister of Education, C. Wallace Whitfield, resigned, followed by two other ministers. Warren Levarity, who had been previously removed from his Ministry, and Maurice Moore, the Freeport/East End representative, and some others brought the total of 'rebels' to eight. Though the split was caused more by difference of opinion than fundamental political philosophy the ousted members of the PLP contended that they sought to redress the Freeport situation. The Free PLP, as the splinter party became known, was appointed the official opposition party in the House in 1971 and later it changed its name to the Free National Movement and merged with the UBP.

Excluding some of the quasi-governmental concessions granted to the Port Authority under the Hawksbill Creek Agreement, the Government of the Bahama Islands has, of course, jurisdiction over the Port area in the same way that it has over the remainder of Grand Bahama. However, because of the special nature of

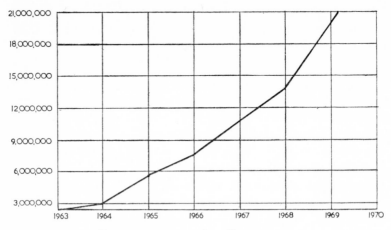

Government revenue from Freeport area

Freeport the prime minister has 'relations with the Grand Bahama Port Authority' listed as one of his responsibilities. Other responsibilities of the chief executive include external affairs, statistics, police and the Prime Minister's Office which covers such matters as co-ordination between the various ministries and the law courts.

The only law court on the island is the Magistrate's Court in Freeport, though local commissioners can pass judgement on minor offenders. The Royal Bahamian Police are represented in every settlement on the island and they also have a Criminal Investigation Department (CID) in Freeport. The police in Grand Bahama, as in the Bahamas as a whole, are well known for their distinctive appearance, courtesy and efficiency. The unpopular but essential task of immigration control of the Bahamas is the responsibility of the Ministry of Home Affairs. This Ministry is responsibile for the control of immigration for the entire island by the issue of residential and work permits for the expatriate population. The Ministry of Finance also maintains a small office in Freeport. It is noteworthy that revenue derived from Freeport in the form of fees, customs duties, etc., amounted to nearly $20 million (1969 and represented a major source of revenue to the public treasury of the Bahamas.

166

In addition, in Freeport the Government maintains a news bureau, a labour office, and public health department and a department of public works. The Ainsley Clinic at West End is a Government-owned and operated facility, for a time in the charge of the devoted District Medical Officer, Dr Richter, and there are other clinics (built by the Port Authority under the terms of the Amendment Agreement, but operated by Government) at Hawksbill and Eight Mile Rock. In Freeport the Government took over the administration of the sixty-five-bed Rand Memorial Hospital in 1970 and there are, in addition, two private medical clinics. To aid the overworked medical officers on the island a district nurse has been in residence at McLean's Town since 1962.

Education is compulsory in the Bahamas to the age of fourteen. There are schools in all the major settlements though a fair amount of overcrowding is apparent. In September 1969 there were a total of 3,615 students enrolled in the fourteen Ministry of Education schools on Grand Bahama. There are some small parochial schools in Eight Mile Rock and the Catholics run a primary school at Hunter's attached to the church of St Vincent de Paul. In Freeport the Government maintain an all-grade school of twenty-six classrooms with six elective classes at Hawksbill, and also in Freeport the Methodists administer St Paul's, a primary school; the Roman Catholics run Mary Star of the Sea primary school and a high school at Hawksbill, and the Lutheran church maintains another primary school. The Port Authority built, and helps subsidise, the seventeen-classroom Freeport High School and also provided the land and helped finance almost all the school building in the Port area.

THE PRESS

The Bahamas have a flourishing publishing business. Besides two daily newspapers, and several twice-weekly and weekly papers, a great amount of 'glossy' literature is published in the Bahamas. The best general publication is the *Bahamas Handbook and*

Businessman's Annual which follows a similar format every year with features and information on the Bahamas in general, a chapter on the Government and a Freeport section.

The first newspaper was the American-owned *Freeport News*, first published on 25 March 1960. This newspaper started by being a weekly but in 1971 started publishing five editions each week. The *Nassau Tribune* started publishing a daily section on Freeport in 1966 and then in 1968 they came out with the *Grand Bahama Tribune* which, though it shared pages with the Nassau edition, became the first daily paper to be published in Freeport. The *Tribune* later reverted to its original form though it features prominently news from Grand Bahama. The editor of the *Tribune* is a remarkable Bahamian, Sir Etienne Dupuch. A sound reformer and once a political radical (he was once critical of the Duke of Windsor when he was governor of the Bahamas), he was instrumental in accelerating the pace of desegregation in the colony though he is oddly out of fashion in the Bahamas of today in that he maintains a strong loyalty to Britain and is exceptionally critical of the winds of change blowing through the islands.

FUTURE PROJECTS

To further their expressed intention of coming to grips with Freeport, the Government have stated that they intend to create a Civic Centre which would centralise the governmental office accommodation and physically demonstrate its presence in Freeport. In addition, the Bahamas Radio Station ZNS plan to construct a studio building on an adjacent site in the central area of Freeport and intend to install antennae and radio masts at West End and High Rock to improve radio reception and eventually they hope to provide a national television service to the island.

In order to reduce the reliance on overseas as a source of food, a large commercial fishing fleet, financed by private enterprise, has been established in Freeport. In 1971 about ten 40ft long ferro-cement boats were constructed at Bahama Terrace which

were intended to form the nucleus of the fishing fleet. It is anticipated that further boats will be built in Freeport and a fish-
processing plant will be constructed in the near future.

The Port Authority for their part have indicated that they are
studying the feasibility of expanding and deepening Freeport
harbour and possibly creating another deepwater harbour and
related industrial zone at the eastern end of the island. They are
also preparing plans for the building of an 'airpark' industrial
area which would permit aircraft to taxi-up to specially built
factories and warehouses. This project should make it feasible
for Freeport to become a 'forward warehouse' for European
goods and a two-way 'gateway' to the Commonwealth for foreign
manufacturers and in line with this aim in 1970 one British air-
cargo firm started flying a regular schedule to and from the
United Kingdom. With a strong industrial infra-structure already
in existence most forms of industry which are not labour-intensive
should continue to establish on the island. The north shore of the
island will eventually be developed with a network of waterways
though part of the area has been recommended to be conserved
as a wild-life sanctuary. In the centre of the island a 500 acre
tract has been proposed for use as a zoological garden which
might feature a man-made hill and serpentine lake.

Studies have also been made into the possibility that Grand
Bahama could be connected to the island of Abaco by a series of
causeways leapfrogging between the existing sandspit islands. To
reduce the length of the causeways fixed span bridges might be
used in addition to artificial islands which might later be developed
for housing or as tourist centres. Such a link would be of tremend-
ous value to both islands. The first link in such a project has been
the construction of twenty-one miles of the Grand Bahama Highway from Freeport to Gold Rock Creek which is planned for
future extension eastwards. Besides opening up land communications with the east end of the island the highway project is an
interesting illustration of co-operation between the Government,
the Port Authority and the Development Company, who jointly
financed the construction. Later, it is quite possible that a rapid

transit system of the monorail type might be installed between the airport and the principal tourist foci of Freeport.

Other private ventures include the construction of studio facilities near Buckingham County area. Already one full length film, *Chokeberry Bay*, starring Allan Alda, has been filmed on the island at West End and from a taxation, as well as a climatic, point of view, other film-makers should find the island to their liking. A strange project, begun in 1971, was the sinking of an underwater sea laboratory in about fifty feet of water off Lucayan Beach. This project is a non-profit venture financed by Mr Perry of Perry Publications (publishers of the *Freeport News*) and Wallace Groves. The purpose of the laboratory is to gain information from the sea and also to test the feasibility of human submarine existence. Already people have lived for a week on the bottom of the ocean and experiments are continuing. In the future, if the population explosion of the world continues and it becomes necessary to create more land, part of the shallows of the Little Bahama Bank might be reclaimed. Alternatively the Bank would be an ideal site, geographically and climatically, for a 'floating city' possibly using some of the information gained from the sea laboratory experiments to make it livable.

The Freeport venture has awakened the interest of other real estate developers in the Bahamas. *Newsweek* magazine suggested that the sheer excitement created by the Grand Bahama 'explosion' had caused subsidiary booms all around the islands—the biggest in terms of capital outlay being Paradise Island near Nassau, though other large projects are proposed or underway in Abaco, Bimini, Eleuthera and San Salvador. It is noteworthy, however, that nowhere else in the Bahamas, except for Paradise Island, has a gambling licence been issued.

PROSPECT FOR THE FUTURE

The phenomenal development which Grand Bahama enjoyed in the late 1960s saw the making of many fortunes. Besides the dozen or so millionaires who invested in the island, some businessmen, large and small, have seen their assets double and treble in as many years. In the early days particularly, Freeport enjoyed an unbridled form of private capitalism; government was by contract, immigration was virtually unrestricted and not a single tax was levied except a modest import duty on consumable items. Small wonder the early pioneers wish to put the clock back. But despite the setbacks to the Freeport economy, the future still promises much. As an indication of the faith that investors still place in the island the sale of land in the vexatious year of 1970 was little short of miraculous with a gross income close to $32 million.

It is not the purpose of this book to interpret the political situation of the Bahamas and its possible effect on Grand Bahama, but nor can it ignore that important political moves are underway which will have far-reaching effects throughout the Bahama Islands and even the world outside. Of primary importance is the move towards independence which should be a reality in 1973. As part of the move towards nationalism is the awakening of racial pride and the stress on social and economic development. In the democratic milieu of the Bahamas the timing and method of carrying out these programmes, though not the principles themselves, have of course found their critics. To counter the poor publicity of 1970 and the faltering confidence in the Bahamas, the Ministry of Development instituted a newsletter, *Bahamas Economic Report*. The first issue came bluntly to the point : 'Because the government is black, one is led to believe that the leaders must be Black Power advocates; because the government has tried to train and upgrade blacks one is led to believe that whites are not welcome; because there was a recession in the US in 1970, the tourist figures were slightly lower, and one is led to believe that bad government must be the cause. We in the Bahamas know differently and are extremely confident of our future.'

It is clear that the Bahamas, perhaps even more than the other Caribbean islands, are caught in the nexus of economic dependence on the West. A Jamaican writer put the dilemma succinctly :

'This whole part of the world, particularly with its close proximity to the USA is sold . . . beyond any possibility of retreat, on the absolute desirability of a Western-type civilisation though there may be no positive understanding of what it involves.' Certainly with few natural resources the Bahamas is almost totally dependent on North America, with the 'invisible export' of tourism and the tangible export of commodities like oil products, cement, crawfish and lumber. The result is that the Bahamas has a balance of trade deficit with the United States, spending more for goods and services than it receives in revenues from direct exports to the United States. In currency crises the Bahamas, though part of the sterling area, twice opted to 'peg' the Bahamian dollar with its United States counterpart, though in 1972 it revalued 5 per cent upwards against the US dollar. Nevertheless a residual British influence persists in the Bahamian educational system, the administration of law and justice and even in the custom of driving on the left-hand side of the road (albeit in left-hand drive cars). As the Bahamians become more self-assertive, however, the slender ties with the mother country will doubtless become even less.

Unfortunately, the Bahamas are apt to be lumped together with other Caribbean islands, when the region receives negative publicity, as, for instance, in the 'Black Power' troubles in Trinidad. But despite the racial bias of a few elements in the society (white and black), the country has been spared overt forms of racialism, and so far the cry of foreign 'exploitation' has hardly been heard. Though it is clear that the country will only maintain its tax-free status if foreign companies doing business in the Bahamas prove that they understand their position and voluntarily help improve the social and economic life of the nation. Thus the country walks a tightrope balanced between economic prosperity and foreign economic domination on the one hand, and a domestic enterprise 'fishing village' economy on the other. Though it is to be hoped that a compromise can be reached which will provide for increasing Bahamian participation within a stable society, in which contracts are honoured and investment is encouraged.

172

Earlier it was indicated that with the change of government of the Bahamas a new economic policy is in the process of being forged. The Bahamian in Freeport is no longer 'the victim of an unbending social order' but a vital, if recent, member of most institutions and businesses. In some part this has been brought about by immigration policy, but to an even greater extent by the Bahamians' own ambition and will to succeed. Although but recently politicised, the Bahamian has moved in a few years from a co-operative to a competitive mode of existence. The Government sensibly instituted a policy whereby a significant part of the companies being formed in the country will be made available at a first offering to Bahamians to encourage local participation in business ownership. And on the cultural side, the Government has encouraged the establishment of a branch of the University of the West Indies to the Bahamas as well as actively fostering the study of the arts and the Bahamian cultural heritage. The future contribution of Grand Bahama might well be to act as a catalyst between the old and the new.

Certainly, when Grand Bahama is reviewed in economic terms in its Bahamian context it is clear that it offers an alternative to the present reliance on tourism as the mainstay of the economy. There is for instance the possibility that North Americans may change their travel habits to the detriment of the Bahamas. In 1970 the Bahamas experienced, for the first time since the war, a slight falling off of the number of expected visitors, which implied that the economic recession in the United States had had an effect. Besides tourist spending was down, which suggests a change in the character of the tourist market. The year 1971, however, reversed the trend and there was a 12·7 per cent increase over 1970.

The great unresolved question, however, is the role the Government will play in the future of Grand Bahama. The Hawksbill Creek Agreement has been likened to the charters of the great trading companies of the former British Dominions and there is unquestionably some similarity in the intent and purpose in these charters. The trading companies were commissioned to trade and colonise their respective territories, but when the companies became sufficiently large they were made subject to political control by the territorial government. There is no question that the Bahamian Government considers the time has come to effect 'political control' and establish a presence in Freeport. Basically 'foreign' to the Bahamian way of life, Government spokesmen claimed that Freeport had become a 'country within a country'. Despite efforts to encourage a Bahamian image in Freeport physically the community is more akin to South Florida than to the Bahamas and, before the strict control on immigration, the Bahamian in Grand Bahama was in danger of becoming a minority on a Bahamian island. In its favour the Bahamas has a racial harmony which could serve as a model to the world, but how the vital immigration problem will be handled is critical for the future. Almost all the land sales of the island have been made to 'expatriates' who, if they were permitted to move to the Bahamas in the near future, would outnumber the native Bahamians in the entire country in a ratio of about four to one. Clearly this is a political problem. To permit unrestricted immigration would create an untenable problem of sovereignty if foreign citizens outnumbered Bahamians though economists agree that the Bahamas are underpopulated in comparison with their economic potential and need to attract foreign manual and skilled workers.

In retrospect, the Freeport venture's most important consequence may well be its catalysing effect on the political aspirations of the Bahamas. It made an issue of foreign immigration, and although it invited sensationalist journalism on matters of politics, race and gambling, it nevertheless spurred the Bahamian people to a national awareness which, inevitably, lead them to seek independence from Britain. It is probable, however, that independence will have less effect on Grand Bahama than will the attitude taken by Government to its foster-child, Freeport. If present achievements are reinforced, Grand Bahama could well become a premier Caribbean region industrial and resort centre. The stage is set, even though confidence seems to be faltering.

Now might be a good time for all entrusted with the island's future to heed the wisdom engraved on the statue in Churchill Square :

> If we pick a quarrel between the past and the present,
> We shall find that we have lost the future.

AN ISLAND GAZETTEER

In 1925 the Government published a map-book of the Bahamas in which were listed the settlements of Grand Bahama. The representation of the shape and size of Grand Bahama was about as inaccurate as that produced on maps of the island three centuries previously; however, the map-book is an interesting reference for the settlements of the time. There was, of course, no settlement on the eastern bank of Hawksbill Creek where Freeport stands today, though the site of Freeport was enigmatically designated in large print as 'FAIRFIELD'. Local inhabitants at the time confirm that there was nothing in the way of development to merit the special reference. For the meagre population of the island—about 2,000—there was a surprising number of communities on the island, each of which was identified by name. Almost all of the settlements indicated in the map-book still exist today. The following is a brief description of villages established before World War II, as one travels from west to east.

West End

Unlike the other communities of the island, West End had little agricultural potential but this was compensated for by its fishing industry and its function as a port of call. The village today consists essentially of two roughly parallel roads with four or five link roads between. The north esplanade, named Bay Shore Road, runs along the sea coast and is the principal street of the village. It is lined with bars, a two-storey framed hotel of World War II vintage, churches and residences. On the seaward side of the

L

road there is a straw market, docks, boatyards and small mountains of conch shells. On the other side of the road the General Seafood factory, built during the war, is still standing, though it is in a sadly dilapidated condition. The Prohibition era Seamen's Club, opposite to D & L Bar, is also closed to business. Helweg Larsen suggested that West End is a place 'where the moon seems more romantic somehow, the colours streak the sky a little deeper hue and the soft evening breezes are gentler than you've ever remembered'. Even though this is only one man's opinion it must be granted that Helweg Larsen knew enough of the world that his judgement should count for something!

The Grand Bahama Hotel is at the western end of the coastal road and today boasts over 500 rooms and a wide range of facilities from an 8,000ft long jet airstrip to skeet shooting, golfing, fish pens, an extensive marina, a sandy beach and shopping arcade. Phil Brinkman, the American artist, has painted some delightful murals in two other facilities of the hotel: the cafeteria and the Witches' Light Bar (the latter incidentally faces the largest swimming pool in the Bahamas).

Visible from West End are the islands of Indian Cay (about a quarter of a mile from the marina channel entrance), Wood Cay and Sandy Cay. Over the horizon further north is the barren islet shown on the early maps of the Bahamas, now a navigation light station known as Memory Rock. At the end of Bay Shore Road the small settlement of Hope Estate marks the eastern end of the Bight and it is here that the coastal road turns inland to join the 'back' road. As one travels eastwards some subdivisions have been developed on land which was originally owned by Grand Bahama Properties. Bootle Bay, Crystal Beach and Buccaneer Beach are three such developments, the latter of which features the Buccaneer Club of Paul Mack, an American who has been on the island since the 'bootlegging' days.

Holmes Rock and Seagrape

Holmes Rock is a village which straggles along the two-lane

178

highway from West End to Freeport known as 'Government' Road or Queen's Highway. The community consists mostly of wooden-framed houses, the whitewashed Mount Olivet Baptist church, a few shops, the Elbow Room Restaurant and the 'Fat Man's Paradise'. Deadman's Reef, nearer the ocean, is part of the same census enumeration district as Holmes Rock, though at the last census it recorded less than fifty people. Almost all villages have numbers of derelict and half-finished buildings which tends to underline the transient nature of many of the communities, and Holmes Rock is no exception.

Seagrape is in reality a small inland 'subdivision' north of Government Road, though the name now refers to a much larger area. Some of the houses in this village were moved from Pine Ridge after 1955. The population of Seagrape was estimated to be about 2,000 people (1969), about 95 per cent of whom were originally Turks Islanders either formerly engaged, or descended from people formerly engaged, in lumbering. At the southern end of the Seagrape subdivision is the Methodist church of St David which was built in 1960. Slightly removed from Government Road on the road leading to the sea front is the modern Roman Catholic church of St Agnes which resembles (some say) the inverted hull of a boat.

Eight Mile Rock

Eight Mile Rock is the name given to nearly eight miles of rocky foreshore west of Hawksbill Creek and geographically includes the villages of Brady Point, Martin Town, Jones' Town, Pinedale and Hannah Hill. The main street is the 24ft wide Queen's Highway which is about a mile inland from the south coast. Almost all the original buildings are of single-storey, wooden-framed construction though a barrel-vaulted school, operated by the Anglicans, is still in use. An ocean-front road is also partly developed with small houses, two small hotels, St Stephen's Anglican church and the former commissioner's office and residence, the latter now in an advanced state of disrepair. A new Government complex has been built on a site near the centre of the community on the coastal road. From an aesthetic point of view Eight Mile Rock may be a candidate for the title of the ugliest community in the Bahamas, yet, paradoxically, it is probably one of the wealthier of the out-island village settlements.

Pinder's Point, Lewis Yard, Hunter's

Like Eight Mile Rock the settlements on the east side of Hawksbill Creek consist of several hardly distinct villages, all strung along a single road. In the extreme west is Pinder's Point which is the most important of the villages, boasting several well-stocked shops and a few churches, including an impressively large Baptist church. Very little of the residential building is in any way distinguished and some of the recent 'housing', if it may be called that, constructed originally for the immigrant labourers, is of very mean appearance. Next along the road is Lewis Yard, named for the Lewis family who once lived in a compound denoted on the 1926 map as 'The Yard'. Here the enterprising Russell family own a service station, commercial premises and a night club and bar (Audley's Recess). Further west is Hunter's which has several small wooden-framed houses and the delightful Catholic church dedicated to St Vincent de Paul. In the extreme east is Mack Town which is named for the incumbent Mack family.

Russell Town and Williams Town

Almost due south of the centre of Freeport is a small village straggling along the sea coast named for the owner/occupiers : the Russells and Williams. A small Catholic church, dedicated to St Jude and built in 1967, is physical evidence of the faith of most of the inhabitants of these villages. A large swamp parallels the beach leaving a strip of dry sandy land some hundred yards wide where the village has been built. The swamp itself is traversed by an old causeway, now sadly overgrown, but of impressive dry rubble masonry construction. Hidden in the pine barren half a mile north of the village are signs of early habitation and an extensive orange grove and some caves which in the past served as fresh-water wells.

Smith's Point and Mather Town

Smith's Point and Mather Town are two small settlements, now separated by a channel inlet from the sea to the Fortune Bay canal system. Both are still served by a sand road and possess only a few wooden and concrete block houses which contrast strangely with the impressively modern (though at present largely unsettled) canal development of the expatriate developers which surrounds them.

In 1968 Smith's Point built a new church which was dedicated by Bishop Markham to replace the Anglican church demolished sometime earlier by the Grand Bahama Development Company in their expansion eastwards. The White Wave Club bids welcome to visitors seeking to shoot pool and quench their thirst. In August 1970 a small Baptist church for the Mather Town community, donated by the Development Company, was dedicated at the western end of Fortune Beach.

'Old' Freetown

'Old' Freetown until recently was a straggling village built behind the sand dunes on a particularly beautiful stretch of beach. Though quite small in population, this settlement, about fifteen miles east of Mather Town, was spread out for over a mile. When lumber mill No 8 was in operation some of the workers settled near Freetown and the temporary community became known as 'Racoon Town'. The entrance to the village from Government Road has, for years, been marked by an overturned car.

Water Cay

Water Cay is a small islet situated almost centrally off the north coast of Grand Bahama at a distance of about one and a half miles by sea through the swashland. At low tide the channel to the island is only a few feet deep. The island has a central ridge of some 30ft elevation, running north and south, and is a few hundred yards wide and about a mile long. The community was founded by seven shareholders about 100 years ago and the first two families to move in were the Russells from Peterson's Cay and the Youngs from Freetown. Later they were joined by the Heilds and the Cornishes from Abaco and the Poitiers from Cat Island (the latter being a distant branch of the other famous Cat Island family of the same name). The patriarch of the village is the centenarian the Rev Thomas Heild who recalls that he settled in Water Cay in 1901. At that time there were only two families living there in houses constructed of wattle and plaster. In the early days the chief occupation of the people was the growing of sea cotton and sponging on the Little Bahama Bank. Almost anything grows in Water Cay and it is today perhaps the most luxuriant part of Grand Bahama. The village is built mainly along the ridge line with the Baptist church at the southern end, approached by a paved footpath. The Government dock is on the east side and nearby is the Telecommunications Office, tended by Mr Poitier, the grandson of one of the first settlers. There are no vehicles, bars or shops (to merit the name) on the cay. At the northern tip of the island is a rock in the shape of a pulpit named Blackbeard's (or Greybeard's) Point, since it was here, as tradition has it, that a pirate of that name was captured and killed. The village consists of about 400 inhabitants, many of whom work in Freeport and return home only at weekends, or even less frequently. Despite the fact that it is less than two miles from the 'Freeport area', in mentality it belongs to the old Bahamas.

Gold Rock and Bevin Town

Gold Rock is the modern counterpart of Golden Grove. In 1951 the United States Government built a missile-tracking base camp, a 7,200ft long airstrip and dock adjacent to the (now) 'Port area' boundary. Related installations dot the coastal road for about five miles in the form of giant radar screens ominously pointing vertically upwards, towers, masts, antennae and electronic installations bearing impressive-sounding names of the space age. One such facility is a 'missile destruct' facility designed to 'destruct' a rocket launched from Cape Kennedy which gets out of control. Built two miles east of the tracking station headquarters is Bevin Town, which is an uneven line of buildings built along Government Road, about a quarter of a mile inland from the sea. The Three Sisters Restaurant specialises in native dishes and the Star Club is the best bar for miles. Until recently most of the villagers worked at the Missile-Tracking Station. In 1969 the former residents of Freetown were rehoused in a small subdivision near Gold Rock.

High Rock

High Rock is a small village about five miles east of the Gold Rock settlement. The main Government Road is about a quarter of a mile distance from the sea and fronting this road are the Government Administrative Offices which accommodate the Police Station and the Commissioner's Office. The commissioner lives in a fairly commodious house on the link road to the village. The village proper is built along a coastal road and the link road (Solomon Drive). High Rock gets its name from the 20ft high rocky 'bluff' between the coastal road and the sea. Almost completely unspoiled by the low-cost concrete block residential structures, the village is built mainly of wooden-framed and boarded buildings, one, two and sometimes three deep from the sea. Located along the coastal road (Felix Slope) are the principal churches: the Lighthouse chapel, Church of God, Baptist and Anglican churches. The catechist of the latter is 75-year-old Felix Roberts, after whom the coastal road was named. The principal livelihood of earlier times was sponging on the Little Bahama Bank, which necessitated a five mile walk every morning along a track through the woods to the sponge boat dock on the north shore. Some of the villagers still grow guinea corn, citrus and vegetables besides fishing; others work at the Missile Base and in Freeport.

Pelican Point

On the best white sand beach on Grand Bahama, Pelican

Point village consists of a single road about 100yd inland from the sea. Most of the building is on the north side of the road, the most imposing structure being St Matthew's Baptist church. There is also an unpretentious service station, some typical wood-framed houses, a grocery store and the inevitable 'club'. Persons travelling east on the coast road should stop at Pelican Point to inquire of the state of the road to East End. Shifting sand dunes, tides and puddles make the road all but impassable at certain times of the year. In 1935 a settlement lower down the coast was inundated by the sea and several people were drowned. The remaining settlers moved to Pelican Point and High Rock. Travelling eastwards just after leaving Pelican Point one passes a cemetery. Village cemeteries on the island are always located on the sea shore since elsewhere the digging of graves would create an arduous task. The arched gateway to the cemetery is typical of all the village cemeteries on the island.

Rocky Creek and Thomas Town

Hardly qualifying as a village, Rocky Creek consists of three to four small houses built at the head of a creek near McLean's Town. The patriarch of Rocky Creek is octogenarian Joseph Bevin, who owns an extensive citrus orchard. Married five times, Joseph Bevin has only one arm, but he still fishes and handles a boat with amazing dexterity. Nearby in the creek is a boiling hole so full of fish that it serves as a larder for the Bevins. Thomas Town, a mile along the road, consists of one house owned, appropriately enough, by Mr Thomas.

McLean's Town

McLean's Town is actually located on a cay and has an unreliable supply of ground water which has to be supplemented by piped water from the 'mainland'. It is the last of the villages of Grand Bahama that can be reached by road and consists of two roughly parallel paved roads. The north road boasts a couple of bars. The south road borders Carrion Crow Harbour, named for the carrion-eating 'turkey' buzzard or vulture. A small masonry dock has been built by the Government and the community has a resident nurse at the pink 'Government Clinic'. An Englishman and his wife teach at the two-classroom public school. Israel 'Jolly' Russell (and almost everyone else in McLean's Town) owns a boat and will ferry passengers to the most easterly community of the island—Sweeting's Cay. The villagers are very good fishermen and occasionally bag a turtle as well as the more common type of Bahamian fish. A very commodious Baptist church was dedicated on 2 February 1969. A mile down the road to the east one can hail a ferry for the short crossing to the few modern buildings which comprise Deep Water Cay. This cay has a small airstrip 1,000ft long, a few guest cottages and, of course, a bar.

Sweeting's Cay

The approach to Sweeting's Cay is by way of a narrow channel which has a lighted marker maintained by the Imperial Lighthouse Service. Sand bars are on either hand and the draught at low tide is not much more than a foot, so a guide is recommended. Sweeting's Cay has the reputation of being the cleanest community on the island and this may well be true. Almost every house sits in a yard of swept white sand bordered by conch shells. The village is located on the western bank of Sweeting's Cay Creek and extends for nearly a mile, built alongside a wide paved footwalk (there are no vehicles on the cay). It was originally settled because of the adjacent sheltered, if shallow, creek and also because it was near to the sponging grounds of the Abaco Bight. When the sponge industry ceased, the villagers gathered and exported shells for a time. The natives today are engaged in fishing or occasionally employed in the nearby expatriate developments of Deep Water or Sweeting's Cay. There are Baptist and Anglican churches in the village and a couple of burial societies meet quarterly. On the lighter side for 'frolic' (as an old-time resident of the cay put it) there are several bars, the principal of which are the Traveller's Rest (specialising in seafood dishes) and the Seagarden Bar (a two-storey building on the waterfront which has a few hotel rooms). Sweeting's Cay is served by the mail boat from Nassau every two weeks. On the west side of the cay is a small development consisting of a guest house and a few cottages owned by 'Mistress Margo' (the Bahamian way of saying Mrs Margo Price).

NOTES ON PLACE NAMES

In the English-speaking world the Bahama Islands have some of the most delightful names ever ascribed to geographical phenomena. Indeed due to the wide publicity these islands have received the very name *Bahama* conjures up romantic notions of a subtropical paradise. The name of the country was actually derived from the island of *Grand Bahama* which in turn is a phonetic translation of the Spanish *Gran Bajamar* or the 'great shallows'. However, by the strangely illogical process by which present day English has come down to us, the shallows of Grand Bahama are part of the 'Little' Bahama Bank and the name 'Great' is reserved for the Great Bahama Bank, colloquially known as the 'mud' southwest of Andros Island. The great variety of names in and around Grand Bahama, for the sake of convenience, may be roughly categorised under four headings.

Descriptive names

West End needs no dissertation on its name since it is the most westerly settlement of the island. On old maps, however, this community was called Settlement Point and on a map published in London by James Wyld in 1841 it was called West Point. Further along the coast we find *Eight Mile Rock* so called on account of the eight miles or so of rocky foreshore on the south coast. Adjacent to Eight Mile Rock is the first through-island waterway of the island, *Hawksbill Creek*, named presumably for the Hawksbill turtle which could be found in the creek before the harbour and causeway were constructed. Several miles north of the island is *Mangrove Cay* near the centre of the Little Bahama

Bank. This islet was perhaps one of the 'flooded islands' reported by Ponce de León on his visit to the northern Bahamas in 1513. Other highly descriptive names to be found on the south coast are *Sharp Rocks*, *Boggy Point* and *Rocky Creek* and these need no explanation. An early Ordnance Survey Map of Grand Bahama pedantically identifies *North Riding Point* as 'Riding Point on the North Side'—Riding Point on the south side of the island is really a misnomer insofar as it hardly is a well-defined 'point' or headland and it is certainly not the place to 'ride out' a storm or act as a navigational aid (a 'riding' rock on which to steer a course). Nearby is an area designated as *The Black Land*, which was probably named for the fairly arable black Bahama loam. *Billy Cay* in Hawksbill Creek recalls not a person, but the billy goats that were once kept there. Small islands to this day form ideal paddocks-without-fences in the out-islands.

Proper names

Another category of names would be those called after people. Powles visiting the island in 1888 remarked on the number of names of Scottish origin, some of which have come down to us today like *Grant's Town*, *Dundee Bay*, *Hamilton Beach* (near West End) and *McLean's Town*. And in fact the names of places on Grand Bahama read like a Bahamian *Who's Who*. Top of the list is *Symonette Cay* (a former premier of the Bahamas); then there are common surnames like *Cooper*, *Pinder*, *Lightbourn*, *Sweeting*, *Smith*, *Higgs*, *Maura*, *Hanna* and *Bain*. The island boasts two *Silver Points* which have nothing to do with silver sand, sea or linings but are named after a man who had a penchant for headlands : (Long?) John Silver. The razed and scarified land where the cement plant stands today was once relatively high land named appropriately *Johnny Hill*. An air of familiarity which suggests joint ownership is discernible in some names like *Ann and Lucy Bay* on the south coast and the *Tom and Jerry Cay* off the north coast. The proper name significant by its absence is that of the founder, pioneer and architect of the Freeport venture : Wallace Groves.

Euphonious names

Euphonious or pleasant-sounding names abound on the island. Take for instance *Phillipi Bay*, near Hunter's, which might have been the landfall of an apostle, or *Caravel Beach*, which despite its name is an 'inland' subdivision of Freeport or *Set and be Damned,* a point on the south coast west of Eight Mile Rock. Then there are the *Big and Little Minny Rocks* and *Barbary Beach*— presumably named for the barbarians who litter the beaches with tin cans and other rubbish. And finally a name which is so ono-matopoeic it needs no explanation : *Lower Crishy Swash.*

Mystery names

A final category are the 'mystery' names or names which have no immediate obvious explanation. Take *Memory Rock,* for in-stance, an exceptionally important landmark thirty miles north of West End, but why 'Memory'? Was it because a mental note of this rock was necessary to position one's self to avoid the perilous *Manatilla Shoals*? And what does 'Manatilla' mean? Who or what is the 'Mott' of *Upper Conch* or *Mott Point*? On a macabre note who is the corpse that *Deadman's Reef* is named for? And finally, a very significant name : *Fortune* or *Lower Conch Point* —why fortune? Was the person who named the point trying to tell us something? It was less than half a mile from this point that in 1964 one of the richest finds of underwater treasure was found by four sea divers. Estimates of the find suggest the 'fortune' as being over two million dollars !

I am indebted to the Editor of the *Tribune* for permission to reproduce the above material which has been condensed from three articles which were originally published in the *Grand Bahama Tribune* in 1968–69.

BIBLIOGRAPHY

Reference books are listed under separate chapters. Where the name of the author or a short title only is given, reference should be made to the chapter under which the work is first listed, denoted by the figure in brackets.

CHAPTER 1

Bahamian Review. 'Possible "Lost Atlantis" found near Bimini', p 34. Nassau, February 1971

LAWSON, E. W. *The Discovery of Florida and its Discoverer Juan Ponce de León.* St Augustine, 1946

MORE, (SIR) THOMAS (by Ralph Robinson). *Utopia.* London, 1955

MORISON, S. E. *Admiral of the Ocean Sea.* New York, 1942 (The most thorough work on the voyage of Columbus)

CHAPTER 2

AGASSIZ, A. *Reconnaissance of the Bahamas.* New York, 1894

BOND, DR JAMES. *Birds of the West Indies.* London, 1960 (Standard reference for birds of the region)

CATESBY, MARK. *Natural History of the Carolinas, Florida and Bahamas.* London, 1731 (There is a copy of this exceptional book under lock and key at the Nassau Public Library)

Freeport-Lucayan Town. Cornell University, Department of City and Regional Planning, Ithaca, 1960

HIGGS, MRS LESLIE. *Bush Medicine in the Bahamas.* Nassau, 1969

MILLSPAUGH and BRITTEN. *Bahama Flora.* New York, 1920

MOSELEY, MARY. *Bahamas Handbook.* Nassau, 1926

MOULDING, MARY BAKER. *Shells at Our Feet.* Chicago, 1967

PHILPOTT, ROSS and SAARINEN. *Report on Ground Water* (unpublished), 1967

SHATTOCK, G. B. (ed). *The Bahama Islands.* Baltimore, 1905 (The most comprehensive biological and social study ever made of the Bahamas)

BIBLIOGRAPHY

SHUTTLEWORTH, FLOYD S. and ZIM, HERBERT S. *Non-flowering Plants.* New York, 1967
ZIM, HERBERT S. and INGLE, LESTER. *Seashores.* New York, 1955
ZIM, HERBERT S. and SHOEMAKER, HURST H. *Fishes.* New York, 1955

CHAPTER 3

CRATON, MICHAEL. *A History of the Bahamas.* London, 1962 (The best book on the history of the Bahamas)
CUMMING, W. *The Southwest in Early Maps.* New Jersey, 1958
CURRY, R. A. *Bahamian Lore.* Paris, 1928
Encyclopedia Americana, Vol 2, 'Arawak'. Chicago, 1962
HELWEG-LARSEN, KJELD. *Columbus Never Came.* London, 1963
JOHNSON, C. *The History of the Pirates.* London, 1726
Karpinski Map Collection. New York Public Library, New York
LAS CASAS. *Tears of the Indians, An account of the voyages and . . .* (by J. Phillips). London, 1655
LAWSON (1)
LOVEN, SVEN. *The Origins of Taino Culture.* Goteburg, 1935
MACKINNON, DAVID. *A Tour Through the British West Indies in the Years 1802 and 1803.* London, 1804
MARTYR, PETER. *De Orbe Novo* (prepared by Michael Lok, Hakluyt). London, 1612
MORISON (1)
PEGGS, A. D. *A Short History of the Bahamas.* Nassau, 1955
SCHOEPF, J. D. *Travels in the Confederation 1783–4.* Philadelphia, 1911
STEVENS, CAPT J. (of Antonio de Herrera). *The General History of the Vast Continent and Island of America.* London, 1726 (Early standard reference on the history of the West Indies in several volumes)
'TEQUESTA'. *Discovery of the Bahama Channel.* South Florida Historical Society, 1948
WYLLY, W. *A Short Account of the Bahama Islands.* London, 1788

CHAPTER 4

BAHAMAS GOVERNMENT. *Official Census Reports* to 1970
BELL, H. McL. *Bahamas: Isles of June.* London, 1936
BURNS, (SIR) A. *History of the British West Indies.* London, 1950
CRATON (3)
GRAND BAHAMA DEVELOPMENT COMPANY. *Title Report: Beach Front Parcels* (unpublished). March, 1968

Powles, L. D. *Land of the Pink Pearl.* London, 1888
Rawson, (Sir) R. *Report on the Bahamas.* London, 1865
Robinson, (Sir) W. *The Bahamas.* Paper published by Royal Colonial Institute, London, 1900
Sharer, Cyrus. *Population Growth in the Bahamas* (unpublished PhD thesis). Michigan, 1955
Stark, J. H. *History and Guide to the Bahamas.* Boston, 1891

CHAPTER 5

Bahamas Government. *Map Book.* Nassau, 1926
Bell (4)
Cottman, Evans. *Out Island Doctor.* London, 1969
Devries, A. D. *Fortunate Isles.* London, 1929
Devries, A. D. *In A Forgotten Colony.* London, 1917 (A book which shows great insight with a wealth of keen observation, including some poignant suggestions on how to attract visitors to the Bahamas)
Klingel, G. C. *Ocean Island.* New York, 1957
Moseley (2)
Official Census Reports (4)
Sheddon (Bishop). *Ups and Downs in a West Indian Diocese.* Norwich, 1930

CHAPTER 6

Armytage, L. F. *The Free Port System in the British West Indies.* London, 1953
Cornell University (2)
Government of the Bahamas Islands. *Hawksbill Creek Agreement,* 1955; *Supplemental Agreement,* 1960; *Amendment Agreement,* 1966; *Report of the Royal Commission of Inquiry Appointed on the Recommendation of the Bahamas Government to review the Hawksbill Creek Agreement* (2 volumes). Nassau, 1971
Rigg, J. Linton. *Bahama Islands.* New Jersey, 1959
Wilder, Robert. *An Affair of Honour.* New York, 1969

CHAPTER 7

Curry (3)
Darragh, Charles. *Newsletter.* 1967 onwards
Dupuch, Etienne Jnr (ed). *Bahamas Handbook.* Nassau, 1961 onwards

BIBLIOGRAPHY

GRAND BAHAMA PORT AUTHORITY LTD. *Progress Reports*, 1964 onwards (The story of Freeport in graphic form)
Hawksbill Creek Agreement, et seq (6)
Nassau Guardian, 1948 onwards
Nassau Tribune (also Grand Bahama Tribune), 1960 onwards (ed. by Sir Etienne Dupuch)

CHAPTER 8

Bahamian Times, 1968 onwards
BAHAMAS, COMMONWEALTH OF, 1969. *Statistical Abstract.* Dept of Statistics, CABINET OFFICE, Nassau, 1970
BENGUET CONSOLIDATED. *Annual Reports*, 1969 onwards
DARRAGH (7)
DUPUCH (7)
Freeport News (7)
GOVERNMENT OF THE BAHAMAS ISLANDS (MINISTRY OF FINANCE) AND THE GRAND BAHAMA PORT AUTHORITY LTD. *Guide to Customs Duties Exemptions and Procedures in Freeport.* 1969
Hawksbill Creek Agreement et seq (6)
Nassau Tribune (7)

CHAPTER 9

BELL (4)
CARIBBEAN AND NORTH ATLANTIC TERRITORIES. *The Bahamas Islands (Constitution).* Order in Council 1963. S.I. 1963 no 2084 HMSO 1964 (and subsequent amendments)
GOVERNMENT OF THE BAHAMAS ISLANDS. *An Act to make Provision Regarding the Entry of Certain Categories of Persons into the Bahama Islands.* Nassau, 1970
GOVERNMENT OF THE BAHAMAS ISLANDS. *Proposals relating to the Establishment of Local Government in the Out Islands.* Nassau, 1968
Hawksbill Creek Agreement et seq (6)
MCCARTNEY, TIMOTHY O. *Neuroses in the Sun,* Executive Ideas, Nassau, 1971
MALCOLM, (SIR) H. *History of the Bahamas House of Assembly.* Nassau, 1921
PROUDFOOT, MARGERY. *Britain and the USA in the Caribbean.* London, 1954
Royal Commission Report (6)

194

BIBLIOGRAPHY

SHARER (4)

WALLACE, SUSAN J. *Bahamian Scene*. Philadelphia, 1970

CHAPTER 10

CORNELL UNIVERSITY (2)

GRAND BAHAMA PORT AUTHORITY LTD. *Proposed Aircraft Mainten-ance and Modification Depot*. Freeport, Bahamas, 1960

Hawksbill Creek Agreement et seq (6)

MORE (1)

SLATER, MARY. *The Caribbean Islands*. Batsford, London, 1968

CHAPTER 11

BENGUET CONSOLIDATED (8)

CARGILL, MORRIS (ed). *Jamaica*. London, 1965

CHECCI & CO. *Tourism in the Commonwealth of the Bahama Islands*. Washington, 1969 (A report in which many ideas are put forward for the development of tourism in the Bahamas)

DUPUCH, (SIR) ETIENNE. *Tribune Story*. London, 1967

FAWKES, RANDOL. *The Bahamas Government*. Nassau, 1966

Freeport News (7)

GOVERNMENT OF BAHAMAS ISLANDS. *Annual Report, Tourism in the Commonwealth of the Bahamas Islands*. Ministry of Tourism (1969 awards); *Bahamas Economic Report*, 1971 onwards (Promises to be an informative publication on the background to political decisions in the Bahamas); Ministry of Development and Ministry of Labour and Welfare. *Summary of some Findings of the Manpower Utilisation Survey Conducted during the First Quarter of 1968*. Nassau, 1968

Nassau Tribune (7)

PHILPOTT, ROSS and SAARINEN (2)

SHARER (4)

Statistical Abstract (8)

EXTRACT OF OFFICIAL REPORTS, REGULATIONS AND LEGISLATION RELATING TO FREEPORT

(1) Government of the Bahamas Islands. *The Hawksbill Creek, Grand Bahama (Deep Water Harbour and Industrial Area) Act*. New Providence, 1955

(2) Government of the Bahama Islands. *Hawksbill Creek Agreement (Principal Agreement)*. New Providence, 1955

(3)   Government of the Bahama Islands. *Hawksbill Creek, Grand Bahama (Deep Water Harbour and Industrial Area) (Amendment of Agreement) Act.* New Providence, 1960

(4)   Government of the Bahama Islands. *Hawksbill Creek Agreement (Supplemental Agreement).* New Providence, 1960

(5)   Government of the Bahama Islands. *The Hawksbill Creek, Grand Bahama (Deep Water Harbour and Industrial Area Amendment of Agreement) Act 1965.* New Providence, 1966

(6)   Government of the Bahama Islands. *Hawksbill Creek Agreement (Amendment of Agreement).* New Providence, 1966

(7)   Government of the Bahama Islands. *The Freeport Byelaws Act, 1965.* New Providence, 1965

(8)   Government of the Bahama Islands, Ministry of Health. *The Freeport (Removal of Refuse) Byelaws 1967.* Nassau, 1967

(9)   Government of the Bahama Islands, Ministry of Health. *The Freeport (Water Preservation) Byelaws 1967.* Nassau, 1967

(10) Government of the Bahama Islands, Ministry of Health. *The Freeport (Removal of Refuse) Byelaws 1967.* Nassau, 1967

(11) Government of the Bahama Islands, Ministry of Works. *The Freeport (Building Code and Sanitary Code) Byelaws 1967.* Nassau, 1967

(12) Government of the Bahama Islands, Ministry of Works. *The Freeport (Control of Advertisements) Byelaws 1967.* Nassau, 1967

(13) Government of the Bahama Islands, Ministry of Communications. *The Freeport (Marina and Inland Waterways) Byelaws 1968.* Nassau, 1968

(14) Government of the Bahama Islands, Ministry of Communications. *The Maritime Affairs and Port Authorities Act. The Freeport Harbour Rules, 1968.* Nassau, 1968

(15) Government of the Bahama Islands, Ministry of Aviation. Regulations made under *The Colonial Air Navigation Order 1961. The Landing Fees (Freeport International Airport) Regulations 1966.* Nassau, 1967

(16) Government of the Bahama Islands, Ministry of Aviation. *The Civil Aviation Act. The Freeport International Airport Rules 1967.* Nassau, 1967

(17) Government of the Bahama Islands, Ministry of Works. *The Anti-Litter (Freeport) Rules 1968.* Nassau, 1968

(18) Government of the Bahama Islands. *The Road Traffic Act, The Road Traffic and Speed Limit (Freeport) Regulations 1969.* Nassau, 1969

(19) Government of the Bahama Islands. *Report of the Commission of Inquiry into the Operation of the Business of Casinos in Freeport and Nassau.* Nassau, 1967

(20) Government of the Bahama Islands. *Report of the Royal Commission Appointed on the Recommendation of the Bahamas Government to Review the Hawksbill Creek Agreement* (2 volumes). Nassau, 1971

(21) Government of the Bahama Islands, (Ministry of Finance) and the Grand Bahama Port Authority Ltd. *Guide to Customs Duties Exemptions and Procedures in Freeport, Grand Bahama Island under the Hawksbill Creek Agreement.* Nassau, 1969

(22) The Grand Bahama Port Authority Ltd. *Rates, Rules and Regulations governing the Seaport Facilities, Freeport, Grand Bahama Island, Bahamas. Freeport,* 1964

(23) The Grand Bahama Port Authority Ltd. *Town Planning Regulations.* Freeport, 1968

(24) The Grand Bahama Port Authority Ltd. *Building and Sanitary Code (including Subdivision and Town Planning Regulations).* Freeport, 1967

ACKNOWLEDGEMENTS

As most human activity has taken place on the island within the last century or so, much of the story of the island lives within the memory of its inhabitants. So, in addition to the written source of material of official records, books and newspaper articles, in an attempt to give a balanced biography of the island, the writer went armed with pad, pencil and tape recorder to reconstruct a picture of the traditional way of life of the villages. The author gratefully acknowledges his indebtedness to those many people who, though unnamed, helped in the preparation of this book. Specifically the writer wishes to thank: Isabelle his wife who offered words of encouragement, Judith Burke, an old friend and colleague who corrected the final draft and made many valuable suggestions, Michael Craton, author of the only recent comprehensive history of the Bahamas, who gave advice on historical sources, Mrs Florence Pyfrom of Nassau who made her files on historical research available, and Miss Isabel Hamilton chief librarian of the Nassau Public Library; on the more recent history: Mr and Mrs Wallace Groves, Major C G Bernard, Mr Grey Russell and Mr Leo Savola who provided many photographs as well as reminiscences of the lumbering operation, Mr George Duncan who worked on the Butlin Holiday Village during its construction and gave a most valuable first-hand account of the venture and subsequent take over. The author also wishes to thank: The British Museum, Smithsonian Institution and University of Florida at Gainsville for help and advice and Dean Burnham Kelly of Cornell University for permission to use the student planning report: *Freeport – Lucayan Town*; Grand Bahamians Mrs Susan Wallace, Mr Audley Russell, Mr Felix Roberts, Mr Lorenzo Smith, Mr David Tait, Mr Jonathon Russell

199

and the 'grand old man' of Grand Bahama, the Reverend Thomas Heild; Dr Richter, formerly of the Ainsley Clinic, West End and Dr Paul Fluck of the Rand Nature Centre who helped especially on the second chapter, and the Grand Bahama Port Authority, particularly Mr Carl Livingston of the Marketing Department; erstwhile typists Jackie Paine, Susan Bernstein, Lois Hunter and Eileen Price; finally thanks are due to Mrs Betty Lockyer who, from the beginning, gave unstintingly of both hard work and enthusiasm in typing the manuscript and later in preparing the index.

INDEX

Abaco, Little and Great, 23, 31, 49, 52, 57, 61, 66, 69, 80, 96, 155, 169–70
Abaco Lumber Company, 80, 84
Administration, 139–40
Admiral of the Ocean Sea, 48
Africa (Africans), 20, 136
Agassiz, A., 30
Air park, 169
Airport(s), 106, 169, 184
Alaminos, 46–7
Allen, Charles, 97
Amendment Agreement, 111–112, 128
An Affair of Honour, 91
Anglicans, 61, 64, 105, 132, 179, 181, 183, 185
Anthem, Josiah, 70
Arawaks, 43–4
Arredondo, Antonio de, 50
Atlantis, 14
Australian pine, 30

Bacon, Francis, 50
'Bahama' (*baja mar*), 46, 49, 51–2, 58, 187
Bahama Cement Company, 103, 106, 110, 145–6
Bahama Channel, *see* Florida Channel
Bahama Flora, The, 31, 68
Bahama Islands, 44
Bahama marl, 24
'Bahamarama', 112
Bahamas Air Sea Rescue Association (BASRA), 162
Bahamas Amusements Ltd, 149
Bahamas Census, 62
Bahamas Economic Report, 171
Bahamas Government, 103–4, 115–29, 139–40, 155–75

Bahamas Handbook and Businessmen's Guide, 79, 95, 100, 167
Bahamas Oil Refining Company (BORCO), 119–20
Bahamas Shipyards Ltd, 95, 145
Bahama stoney loam, 24
Bahamas Timber Company Ltd, 69
'Bahamia', 149
Bahamian pine, see *Pinus caribaea*
Bahamian Scene, 141
'Banana hole', 23
Banks, 163
Baptists, 61, 132, 179, 183, 184–5
Baran, Don Alvaro de, 51
Barbary Beach, 189
Barracuda, 41
Bell Channel Bay, 105, 148
Bell, H. McL., 74–6
Benguet Consolidated Inc, 117–18, 123–7
Bevin Town, 182–3
Big and Little Minny Rocks, 189
Billy Cay, 188
Bimini, 45, 47, 52, 61, 64, 115, 139, 155, 170
Birds, 20, 37–8
'Blackbeard', *see* Teach, Edward
Black Land, The, 188
Blunt, Edmund, 60
Boggy Point, 188
Boiling holes, 26
Bond, Dr James, 37
Bootle (Bay), 63, 101, 178
Bootleggers, 34
Bowe, Felix, 75
Brady Point, 179
Britton & Millspaugh, 31, 68
Buccaneer Club, 178
Buckingham County, 80
Building and Sanitary Code, 152
Bunkering (ship), 98, 109, 145

Bush medicine, 33, 70
Butlin, Billy (Sir), 20, 84–6
Butterflies, 37

Cabot, Sebastian, 50
Canary Islands, 13
Caradon, Lord (Foot, Sir Hugh), 96
Caribbean (Sea), 43, 50
Caribs, 43–5
Carrion Crow (harbour), 64,
Casas, Bartolome de las, 48
Casuarina, see Australian pine
Catesby, Mark, 30
CATV, 162
Causeway (to Abaco), 169
Ceboynas, 43
Cecilia, SS, 66
Celia, Aunt, 70
Certificate of Exemption, 109
Chesler, Louis, 104, 109, 111
China Mail, 106
Chokeberry Bay, 170
Churches, 131–2
Churchill, Sir Winston, 150
Churchill Square, 150, 175
Civil War, American, 60
'Clear-Free Black, Prince', 64
Climate 27–8
Columbus, Christopher, 13, 14, 44
Columbus, Diego, 46
Commerce (and industry), 162–5, 168–70
Commissioner(s), 139
Commission on Gambling, 116
Commonwealth of the Bahamas, 20, 119
Communications, 160–2
Conch, see Strombus gigas
Consolidated Construction, 86–7
Coral, 38
Cornell, University (Report), 27, 100, 146–7
Cornway, Captain, 56
Cortés, Hernando, 47, 110
Cosa, see La Cosa
Cottman, Evans, 81
Craton, Michael, 46
Crawfish, see Panulirus argus
Criminal Investigation Dept (CID), 166
Crown (Crown grants), 20, 62–5

Curly tailed lizard, see Leicephalus carinatus armouri
Curry, R. A., 145

Darraugh, Charles (Newsletter), 119
Deadman's Reef, 179, 189
Deep Water Cay, 159–61
Defries, A. D., 67–70
DeGregory, Harold, 105, 139
Delisle, Guillaume, 49
DeMoyne, 60
De Orbe Novo, 43
Destroyer-Bases Accord, 86, 95
Dialect, 135
Drake, Sir Francis, 51
Duhos, 44–5
Dundee Bay, 188
Dunmore, Lord John Murray (Earl of), 58
Duppie, 137
Dupuch, Sir Etienne, 168

Economist, 113
Education, 103, 167, 172
Eight Mile Rock, 26, 62–4, 68, 70, 81, 111–12, 121–2, 132–3, 155
Electric power, 164–5
Eleuthera, 20, 52, 56, 170
Emancipation, 64, 130, 133
Explorers, 43–8, 50–9

'Fairfield', 177
Fauna, 33–42
Fawkes, Randol, 118, 122
Ferdinand, King, 48
Finders Losers, 110
Firth Cleveland Ltd, 97, 118
Fish (fishing), 38–42, 78–9, 131, 168
Flamingo, 37
Flora, 30–3
Florida, 14, 43, 46, 51, 106, 147, 160, 162, 178
Florida Channel, 14, 29, 46–7, 49–52, 60
Fortune Bay (Hills), 27, 109, 151, 181
Fortune (or Lower Conch) Point, 189
Fountain of Youth, 14, 45–6
Freemasonary, 133
Free National Movement (FNM), 165
'Free port,' 91–3
Freeport, 16, 93–101, 103–13, 115, 118, 123, 142–75

Freeport—Lucayan Town, 146–7
Freeport, MV, 118, 160
Freeport News, 104, 110, 116, 168, 170
Freetown, 26, 63–4, 181
Friendship Shopping Centre, 164
Frigate bird, 37

Galaxy, 105
Gambling (Commission), 74, 109, 115–117
Gazetteer, 177–86
General Seafood Co. Ltd, 79, 178
Geology, 23–7
Gibbons, Cardinal, 65
Gilbert, Sir Humphrey, 50
Golden Grove, 63, 139, 182
Golden Hind, The, 56
Gold Rock (Creek), 63, 87, 96, 160, 169, 182
Goldsmith, C. Gerald, 124
Goombay, 136
Gorda Cay, 56
Gorgonia, 38
Gottlieb, Ejnar, 82
Gran Bajamar, 14, 187
Grand Bahama Citizens Committee, 140
Grand Bahama Development Co Ltd, 104, 110–11, 147–54, 181
Grand Bahama Hotel 78, 81, 101–2, 106, 178
Grand Bahama Island, 13
Grand Bahama Mercantile & Development Co, 74
Grand Bahama, MV, 101, 160
Grand Bahama Port Authority Ltd, 93–101, 103–13, 117–29, 142–54
Grand Bahama Properties Ltd, 85, 101, 178
Grand Bahama Tribune, The, 121, 168
Grand Lucayan Waterway, 141–2
Granger, Wenzel, 96
Grant's Town, 188
Grassquits, Black-faced, 38
Great Britain, SS 99
Great Isaac, 52, 66
Green Cross, 81
Grenville, Sir Richard, 51
Grey, Lord (Sir Ralph), 110–11
Groves, Father Gerald, 132

Groves, Wallace, 22, 81–4, 88, 91, 93, 96, 104, 109, 112, 116–17, 124, 128, 135, 170, 188
Groves, Wallace (Mrs), 93
Gulf Stream 14, 27–9, 67, 98

Haiti (Haitians), 112, 122, 138, 155, 157
Hammock, 26–7
Hannah Hill, 179
Harbour(s), 97–8, 160
Harbour Island, 20
Harvard (John) Library, 105
Hawes, Monsignor, 132
Hawkins, John, 50
Hawksbill Creek, 22, 24, 26, 62, 74, 81, 99, 146, 152, 177, 187
Hawksbill Creek Agreement, 20, 93–100, 103, 118, 129, 142, 161, 163, 165, 173
Hayward, Charles, 97, 99, 112
Hayward, Jack, 99–100
Heath, Sir Robert, 52
Heild, Rev Thomas, 61, 78, 182
Hepburn, Augustus, 76
Hermit crab, 40
Herrera Antonio de, 46–7
Hex, 137
Heyn, Piet, 55, 109
Higgs, Mrs Leslie, 33
High Rock, 87, 132, 168, 183
Hispaniola, 13, 45, 48, 50
Historia de las Indias (History of the Indies), 48
History of the Bahamas, 46
Holmes Rock, 101, 111, 178–9
Homer, Winslow, 67
Hood, Thomas, 51
Hotels, 159–60
Hunter, Joseph, 62
Hunter's 63, 130, 151, 167, 180
Hurricane, 28, 81

Igneri, 44
Imperial Lighthouse Service, 66
Indian Cay, 45, 178
Industry, *see* Commerce (and industry)
Inflation, 164
Insects, 34, 37
Intercontinental Realty Ltd, 151

International Bazaar, 149–50, 164
Isabella, Queen, 13, 48

Jack Tar Hotels, 101, 106
'John Canoe', *see* Junkanoo
Johnson, Luther (Duke), 77
Jones' Town, 179
Junkanoo 138–9

'Karst, Phenomenon', 25
Kates, George, 124
Ker, John, 92
Kimball, J. T., 124
King's Inn (Golf and Country Club), 149
Kirtland's Warbler, 38

La Cosa, Juan de, 48
Land grants, 62–5
Landscaping, 32
Larsen, Helweg, 87, 178
La Vieja, 51–2
Leicephalus carinatus armouri, 33–4
Levarity, Warren, 115, 139, 165
Lewis Yard, 63, 180
Licensee(s), 98–9, 121–3
Limestone, 20, 23, 25, 103, 146
Little Bahama Bank, 23, 41, 45, 49, 60, 66–8, 81, 96, 170, 182, 187
Little Whale Cay, 87
Lizards, 33–4
Local government, 120–1, 128
Locomotives, 83
Loven, Sven, 44
Loyalists, 62–4
Lucaya (Lucayo), 43, 47, 50, 104, 145–75
Lucaya, MV, 112
Lucayan Indians, 16, 43–8
Ludwig, D. K., 94–5, 103, 145, 149
Lukku-cairi, 43
Lumber, 19, 80–4
'Luxury Hotel' (Lucayan Beach Hotel), 103, 106, 109, 148, 159
Lynch, Sir Thomas, 55

Mack, Paul, 77, 178
Mackey Airlines, 106
Magistrate's Court, 166
Mailboat, 160
Manatee, *see* Seacow
Manatilla Shoal, 14, 60, 66–7, 189

Mangrove Cay, 187
Manpower Utilisation Survey, 156–8
Map Book, Government, 177
Maps, 48–51, 60, 67
Marco City, 142
Martin Town, 179
Martyr, Peter, 43
Mary Guildford, 50
Mather Town, 181
McKinnon, David, 58
McLean's Town, 63, 70, 130–1, 160, 167, 184–5, 188
Memory Rock, 46, 48, 56, 178, 189
Miami, 16, 62, 113
Miami News, 85
Millspaugh & Britton, 31
Miruelo, Diego, 46
Missile-Tracking Station, 86–7, 182
Mobley and Ashley (gangs), 65
Moll, Herman, 49
Monarch Butterfly, 37
Moore, Maurice, 115, 122, 139, 165
More, Sir Thomas, 16, 150–4
More's Island, 61, 67, 70
Morison, S. E., 48
Motor Vehicles, 161
'Mud, The', 67
Musgrave, Professor Richard, 120

Names (of persons), 134
Names (places), 187–9
Nassau, 57, 61–2, 70, 84, 92, 133, 137–9, 158, 164, 168, 185
Nassau Bottler, MV 122
Nassau Sponge Exchange, 68
National Coal Board, 82
National Container Corporation (Nat Con), 91, 96–7
Natural History of the Carolinas, Florida and the Bahamas, 30
Newsweek (magazine), 170
New York Times, 109, 127
Northern Star Lodge, 133
North Riding Point, 160–1, 188
Northwest Providence Channel, 14, 21, 98

Obeah, 137–8
Ocean currents, 25–6
Ocean holes, 25–6
Ortelius, 49
Ortubia, 46

Out Island Doctor, 81–4
Ovando, Governor, 47
Owens (Illinois) Company, 96

Paine, Thomas, 55
Pane, Friar, 44
Panulirus argus, 40, 71
Paris, Treaty of, 57
Pearle, 55
Pelican Point, 95, 183–4
Peterson's Cay, 63
Phenny, Governor, 58
Phillipi Bay, 189
Phips, Captain, 56
Pinder's Point, 63, 81, 111, 155, 180
Pindling, Prime Minister Lynden O.,
    109, 118, 122
Pinedale, 179
Pine Ridge, 80, 96–7, 142, 145
Pinus caribaea, 31, 80–4
Pirates, 52–9
Pit props, 82–3
Planning, 142–54
Politics, 165–7
Ponce de León, 14, 45–8, 188
Poole, Rev J. H., 70
Population, 16, 60, 62, 74, 100, 155–
    8, 177
Population Graph, 156
Porel, Jan, 97, 142, 147, 150
Port Area, 93–4, 142, 145, 166–7,
    182
Powles, L. D., 62, 188
Press, The, 167–8
Pride, MV, 77
Principal Agreement, *see* Hawksbill
    Creek Agreement
Progressive Liberal Party (PLP), 113,
    115, 118, 139, 165
Prohibition, 75–8
Projects, Future, 168–70
Prospect for future, 170–5
Psilotum nudum, 32

Queen's Cove, 148, 152

Races, 20, 21, 174
Racoon, 34
Radio, 162, 168
Railway, 80–4, 145
Rainfall, 27–8
Rand, James, 105

Rand Memorial Hospital, 167
Ranfurly, Lord, 87–8, 96, 110
Rawson, Governor, 61, 66
Red Shank Cay, 68
Resettlement, 60–5
Retail Price Index, 164
Revenue, Government, 166
Ribero, Diego, 49
Richter, Dr, 135, 137, 155, 167
Robert Fulton, SS, 96
Rocky Creek, 184, 188
Rogers, Capt Woodes, 57–8, 92
Roman Catholics, 132, 179
Royal Commission **Report** **on** **Free-**
    port, 94, 127
Russell Town, 63, 180
Rut, John, 50

Sammons, Charles A., 101
Samos, SS, 99
Sands, Sir Stafford, 91
Sandy Cay, 46, 178
San Salvador, 13, 14, 43, 170
Sapodilla, 31
Saturday Evening Post, 115
Savage, Peres, 55
Schoepf, J. D., 58
Schools, 167
Seacow, 25, 42
Seagrape, 32, 132–3, 170
Sea Laboratory, 170
Seamen's Club, 178
Set and be Damned, 189
Settlements, 130–41
Shannon, 'Red', 76
Sharp Rocks, 188
Shattuck, G. B. 30
Shepard, Alan Bartlett Jnr, 104
Siboney, 43
Silvera, Douglas, 86–7
Silver Banks, 56
Silver City, 142, 145
Silver Point, 188
Slack, Jack, 110
Slaves, 51, 59, 64, 133
Smith, Joseph, 62–3
Smith's Point, 63, 80, 132, 181
Social   background   (Settlements),
    133–41
Social life (Freeport), 100–1
Southern Cross, 28
Southern Cross (Yacht), 79

INDEX

Sponge (Sponging), 40–1, 66–8, 79
St Agnes' church, 132, 179
Standard Oil, 81
Stapledon, Sir Robert de, 106
St Augustine, Florida, 56
St Mary Magdalene, 132
St Michael's, 132
Stratton, Dr, 82
Strombus gigas, 39, 79
St Stephen's church, 132, 179
St Vincent de Paul, 132, 167, 180
Sunset, 19–20
Supplemental Agreement, 103, 106, 111
Surnames, *see* Names
Sweeting's Cay 87, 131, 150–60, 162, 185–6
Symonette Cay, 188

Taino (Taini), 43–8
Taylor International Inc, 147–9
Teach, Edward ('Blackbeard'), 57
Tears of the Indians, 48
Telephone service, 161–2
Thomas Town, 184
Tiger, HMS, 112
Tom and Jerry Cay, 188
Tordesillas, Treaty of, 47
Tourism, 27, 84–8 91, 158–60
Transport (modes of), 160–1
Treasure, 109–10, 170
Tribune, The, see *Grand Bahama Tribune*
Turin Map, 46, 49
Turks Island(ers), 83, 134, 179
Turtle, 41, 58, 79, 185

United Bahamian Party (UBP), 105, 109, 113, 116, 118
United States Coastguard, 75–8

United States Steel Corporation, 95, 103, 110
Upper Conch or Mott Point, 189
Utilities, 161–2
Utopia, 16, 152, 154

Veajus, see *La Vieja*
Venezuela, 14, 43, 56, 98
Verrazano, Giralamo de, 49
Vespucci, Amerigo, 49
Villages, *see* Settlements
Voodoo, 137
Vulture, 37, 185

Waldseemüller, Martin, 48
Wallace, Susan, 113, 141
Wall Street Journal, 113
Wappen von Hamburg, MV 112
Water (potable), 20, 29–30, 111, 165
Water Cay, 131, 162, 181–2
Weather, *see* Climate
Wenner-Gren, Axel, 79
West End, 45, 55, 60–1, 63, 70, 75–9, 81, 84, 101, 106, 121, 132, 141, 155, 159–60, 162, 164, 167–8. 177–8, 187
West Indies (West Indians), 138, 140–1
White, John, 51
Whitfield, C. Wallace, 165
Wilder, Robert, 91
William's Town, 180
Witchcraft, 137–8
Wooley, Captain, 56
Wrecks/Wrecking, 16, 65–8
Wyld, James 187

Zemis (Zemes), 44
ZNS, *see* Radio